Attitudes of
gratitude
—IN—
LOVE

Attitudes of gratitude in LOVE

Creating More Joy in Your Relationship

M. J. RYAN

Foreword by Daphne Rose Kingma,
author of *True Love*

CONARI PRESS

Cover Illustration: Roger Montoya
Cover Design: Claudia Smelser
Book Design: Suzanne Albertson
Interior Illustrations: Roger Montoya

Library of Congress Cataloging-in-Publication Data

Ryan, M. J. (Mary Jane), 1952-
Attitudes of gratitude in love : creating more joy in your
relationship / M. J. Ryan ; foreword by Daphne Rose Kingma.
p. cm.
ISBN 1-57324-765-0
1. Love. 2. Gratitude. 3. Man-woman relationships. I. Title.
BF575.L8 R93 2002
306.7--dc21
2002003510

Printed in Canada.

02 03 04 05 TC 10 9 8 7 6 5 4 3 2 1

The world is not a playground; it's a schoolroom. Life is not a holiday but an education. And the one eternal question for us all is how better we can love.

—HENRY DRUMMOND

Attitudes of gratitude in LOVE

6
_____

THE JOYFUL JOURNEY 193

I have always believed that gratitude is the saving grace in any intimate relationship. A simple "Thank you," a heartfelt "I appreciate," a thoughtful "I'm so grateful . . ." all bring a quality of joy and a sense of belonging to the people who give and receive them. In their humble, gracious way, expressions of gratitude enliven any relationship. Given that this is true, that we can feel better—happier, more optimistic, more connected, and more joyful—through these simple expressions of appreciation, it's amazing how rarely we communicate our gratitude, and remarkable that in fact we need to be reminded, instructed to do so.

One of the reasons for this is that the emotional state of gratitude is, in itself, an experience of vulnerability. We don't feel grateful or say "Thank you" for something that wasn't needed, isn't valued, or doesn't fill an emptiness of some kind. We don't often think of gratitude as exposing our vulnerability in this way, but the truth is, the person who has gratitude to express has in some sense been lifted from a place of lack or need to a place of well-being and abundance. Through a gracious word or deed on the part of another, a wound has been dressed, an emptiness filled, a moment of being enhanced. So it is that when we express our gratitude, we can become aware, in a single instant, both of our own needs and of another's generosity in filling them.

It's uncomfortable to feel vulnerable, though, and so we'd often just as soon receive the gift—whatever it is— without further exposing ourselves by also saying "Thank you." As a consequence, we tend to operate from a taking-it-for-granted rather than a taking-it-in-gratitude mode in our relationships. And unfortunately, it's often the closer the relationship, that the more lax we become about giving voice to our gratitude. We're happy to have the car fixed, the dinner made, the travails of the workday listened to, the mother-in-law carted off to her doctors' appointments—and to see all these simply as the natural functions of a relationship. But when we respond to these extraordinary ordinary gifts with thanksgiving, our appreciation returns a gift to the giver, forms a new strand of connection, and strengthens the weave of our bond.

In this sense gratitude isn't just good manners, it is relationship building. For when we are grateful, we acknowledge both the truth of our needs and the miracle that they have been addressed. And the more we live with a conscious awareness of both of these, the more we are able to see exactly *how* we love one another—and how much we are loved in return.

Gratitude is a powerful instrument for change. That's because each time you express it, your brain erases a little bit more of the patterns it holds of feeling deprived—of being unheard, unheld, un-felt-with, or alone. Every valley exalted by gratitude will stand as a mountain of hope in your heart. And the ongoing expression of your gratitude will be a constant reminder that you are blessed by your relationship, that life is benevolent and kind.

In this lovely book, M. J. Ryan shares her own steps on the path of gratitude. In so doing she offers a wonderful teaching in the hows and whys of thanksgiving for your own relationship. I hope you will enjoy it as the gift it is, and receive it with a grateful heart.

THE KEY TO LIVING
OUR LOVE

Most married couples, even though they
love each other very much in theory,
tend to view each other in practice as
large teeming flaw colonies, the result
being that they get on each other's nerves
and regularly erupt into vicious emotional
shouting matches over such issues as
toaster settings.
                    —DAVE BARRY

*I*N THE THREE YEARS SINCE I wrote *Attitudes of Gratitude*, I've been teaching about and practicing gratitude on a daily basis. What I've come to see is that while it is easy to be grateful in the abstract—for sun and rain and good food—often the place where it is most difficult to practice is in our most intimate relationships. So many of us are (rightfully) grateful to the stranger who helps us pull our car out of the ditch but take for granted the daily gift our loved one is.

I know that's true for me. I am almost always unfailingly appreciative of everyone except the one closest to me. With my husband, just as Dave Barry points out, I spend most of my time cataloging his most irritating foibles and lacks. And yet I know all the way down to my bones that one of the best ways to create happiness and joy in life, and therefore in love, is to be as grateful as possible.

And so I set out to study the phenomenon. What holds us back from a full sense of gratitude to this other being who has chosen us among all others to spend a life with? What would happen if we truly allowed ourselves to feel the gift this love represents? How can we cultivate gratitude for love on a daily basis?

As with all my books, I must say that I am no expert in this. In fact, when it comes to an attitude of gratitude in love, I am a rank beginner. What you are holding in your hand is a work in progress. It represents what I and others have learned about the joy that can be experienced by living in a state of gratitude for our intimate partner; why we keep ourselves from experiencing the happiness gratitude can bring; the attitudes that foster such positive feelings; and the practices that enhance the possibility on a daily basis. I offer it in the spirit of a fellow traveler, one who seeks to live fully and love well, a flawed human being who, at the end of her life, wishes to be able to be proud of the ways she has loved those who have graced her life.

Creating a happy relationship is no small task. It has many components, only one of which—showing gratitude—will be looked at here. But the task itself is very worthwhile. Here's just one way to think about it—in terms of dollars (although how they figure out these things is beyond me). A twenty-five-year study of happiness done by Dartmouth College and London University found that a stable, long-term relationship was equal to $100,000 a year in income in creating happiness! So there's one reason to practice.

Here's another, more spiritually oriented one. I know only a few things with absolute certainty. One is that our intimate relationship—the pairing of one human being with another—is the greatest vehicle for emotional and spiritual growth life affords us. Within its crucible, every old wound is revisited, every certainty is challenged, every fine quality of our being is forced to expand beyond our perceived limits. If we do it right, we are inevitably transformed into more loving and wise human beings. But too often we get stuck in ruts that prevent us from allowing this alchemical magic to take place. We run the same negative stories over and over, we get caught in games of blame and shame, we give up in despair.

That's where the power of gratitude comes in. The more we can practice gratitude for our love, the less we get stuck in the places where relationships can really hang us up. Theorists call this an "asset focus." Increasingly, those who study human systems are doing work that shows the more you look at what's right instead of what's wrong, the more change actually occurs. Impasses break up, new insights arise, and the energy begins to move in a positive direction. Conversely, when you focus on what's wrong, you tend to dig yourself into a bigger hole.

Socially, this understanding of how important an asset focus is can be seen in the switch so many people are making from therapy to coaching when needing support. Therapy assumes you or your relationship are broken and need to be fixed; most of the focus during the sessions is on analyzing the problem and where it came from. Coaching, on the other hand, assumes you or your relationship are whole and supports you in manifesting more of what you want. The current focus on coaching represents, whether implicitly or explicitly, an understanding that noticing what's right is more useful than analyzing what's wrong in creating satisfaction and peace of mind in ourselves and our relationships. This is not to say that therapy or looking at a problem is always bad; sometimes it is crucially important in order to heal. But it is an awareness that perhaps we've been putting most of our attention on the wrong thing. As the song says, We've been looking for love in all the wrong places.

My understanding of this was first born years ago, when a prospective author met with me in my role as executive editor of Conari Press. I am sorry that I can't remember her name to thank her directly, but unfortunately her name is lost somewhere in the annals of my brain. What I do recall is that she was a therapist who had a book idea she wanted to talk with me about. We had lunch, the typical venue for such conversations, and she said to me, "I have the secret to instantly improving any relationship. It's so simple it's almost unbelievable. Anyone can do it, anytime, anywhere, even if only one person in the relationship does it. The other person doesn't even have to know you are doing it." We had a pleasant lunch, and then she went on her way. I never heard from her again. I don't know whether she ever did write her book.

Meanwhile I published hundreds of other books and began to write my own—on kindness, gratitude, simplicity, and generosity. Then one day, after *Attitudes of Gratitude* was such a hit, Conari Press Sales Director Brenda Knight said to me, "I know what you should write about next—*Attitudes of Gratitude in Love.*" That sounded just right, particularly given the learnings I needed in that precise area, so I said yes. Months later, after much cogitating on the topic, the long-ago lunch with the therapist floated into my mind. For—you might have already guessed it—her idea was the practice of gratitude as a sure-fire way to improve any love relationship. So I bow in thanks to her and to the mysteries of the universe that have brought me to this awareness in my own time and in my own way.

As I practice thankfulness and work with others, I've come to know how deeply true it is that gratitude can make any relationship more joyful and enriching. No matter how you feel right now about your partner, your outlook and therefore the situation itself will get better if you simply begin to notice what's already wonderful about him or her. An attitude of gratitude will not solve all problems—no one thing could ever do that—but it can make all problems more manageable. That's because gratefulness is a mood elevator; by flooding our bodies with endorphins, it gives us hope. Gratitude also opens our hearts and gets us out of bitterness or resentment, creating a sense of emotional generosity toward the one we love. And from that place of generosity, new possibilities emerge.

The process is so effective that often I find myself in awe. Love with all of its problems seems to be so complex, how could this be so easy? *Could* it be this uncomplicated? The only thing I can recommend is to experience it for yourself. This little book is a place to begin.

May you find within its pages thoughts and practices that will be stunningly simple for you to use to bring more joy and peace into your most intimate relationship. May your love grow exponentially as you practice, and may the ripples of that love reach out to touch all those around you.

THE GIFTS OF
RELATIONSHIP
GRATITUDE

Kindness in words creates confidence;
kindness in thinking creates profoundness;
kindness in feeling creates love.
—LAO-TZU

WE BEGIN BY LOOKING at what thankfulness and appreciation can do for relationships and the people within them. By focusing on the rewards first, by understanding the benefits of thankfulness, we give ourselves an incentive to begin to learn new attitudes and behaviors. The gifts of gratitude are many, but in some senses, they all boil down to Lao-tzu's quote—gratefulness creates kindness in feeling, which in turn generates more love. And isn't that what we all truly want?

You'll Feel Closer and More Loving

Love doesn't make the world go round.
Love is what makes the ride worthwhile.

—FRANKLIN P. JONES

As I write, Christmas is rapidly approaching, with all of its usual hectic joys and obligations. Add to that three December birthdays in our family—on the 17th, the 20th, and the 25th—a rapidly approaching book deadline, and the fact that I was just away in Europe for a week doing work—and you might not be surprised to know that I've been racing around like a whirling dervish. And given the circumstances, you also probably wouldn't be surprised to hear that my husband and I have barely uttered two words to one another in almost four weeks. Running along on parallel tracks, trying to do everything that needs to get done, we've lost all sense of why we are together.

Last night, in the midst of all my busyness, I noticed that Don had taken our five-year-old daughter Ana aside and was teaching her how to weatherproof her boots in preparation for the trip to Utah we are taking. It was so Don—the quietness with which he had noticed what needed to be done (I would never in a million years have thought to weatherproof her boots) and was just doing it without making a big deal out of it; the patience with which he was showing Ana how to do it; his willingness to even let a five-year-old near the stuff; his praise of her for doing a great job.

Suddenly I was flooded with a sense of immense gratitude that he was in my life, and immediately felt more connected than I had in weeks. I stopped what I was doing and came over to put my arms around him. We then shared a few moments that got our relationship humming again.

Spiritual teachers, particularly of the Eastern variety, are always talking about "waking up." This has many dimensions, but the way that I understand it best has to do with recognizing the beauty of what is right before our eyes. That's what gratitude does. It wakes us up to the ordinary, allowing us to see it for what it truly is, rather than just taking it for granted.

That's what happened to me last night. Don has been going around being Don all along. But because, for that one moment, I woke up and saw Don, I could experience how grateful I am that I have such a wonderful human being to share my life with. And once I felt gratefulness to him, I instantly felt more loving in return.

When you practice gratitude in your relationship, you can't help but feel more connected and loving. It's an inevitable consequence of focusing on what you appreciate about the other person. That's because in reminding yourself of what's so great about the other, you want to draw closer and offer yourself to this marvelous creature who miraculously has chosen you above all others.

You're More Likely to Stay Together

Happily married people aren't smarter, richer, or more
psychologically astute than others. But in their day-to-day
lives, they have hit upon a dynamic that keeps their
negative thoughts and feelings (which all couples have)
from overwhelming their positive ones.

—JOHN GOTTMAN

John Gottman is a relationship expert. Professor of psychology at the University of Washington, he has, over the past twenty-five years, done the most extensive and rigorous scientific research ever conducted into what makes for healthy marriages. Along the way, he has debunked many relationship myths, including the notion that fighting is what causes divorce (it actually depends on how you do it and how well matched your conflict styles are); that common interests will keep you together (not if you mistreat one another in their pursuit); and that men and women are from different planets and have fundamentally different needs (*au contraire*, says Gottman—the determining factor in whether both men and women feel satisfied with the sex, romance, and passion in their marriage is, by 70 percent, the quality of their friendship).

His research all points to one thing—that happy relationships are founded on deep friendships that have a "positive sentiment override. This means that [couples'] positive thoughts about each other and their marriage are so pervasive that they tend to supercede their negative feelings." This positivism, Gottman maintains, "causes them to feel optimistic about each other and their marriage, to assume positive things about their lives together, and to give each other the benefit of the doubt."

When I first read Gottman's research, as articulated in *The Seven Principles for Making Marriage Work,* it was as if I had found the Holy Grail. I had known intuitively that an attitude of gratitude was a great way to create and sustain happiness in love, but Gottman's rigorous research proves it. And it points to the underlying reason why—that practicing thankfulness increases our "positive sentiment override," giving us the emotional resiliency to get through hard times together. In other words, the more we focus on what we appreciate in our mate and articulate that to him or her, the larger our positive emotional bank account will grow, ready to be drawn upon in conflicts big and small.

This is no small thing. Many relationships end, maintains Gottman, because "neither spouse recognizes its value until it is too late. . . . Too often a good marriage is taken for granted rather than given the nurturing and respect it deserves and desperately needs."

Gratefulness in love reminds us why our relationship is important and prevents us from taking the other person and the relationship itself for granted. In some fundamental way it is breakup insurance—what better reason to practice than that!

19

ful that Don realized that my carpal tunnel has gotten so bad that I can't use a manual can opener any more." (Which was the real reason he gave me such a gift.)

When we believe our feelings are a true reflection of reality, rather than our own personal reaction to a situation, we hold on tightly to our negativity and don't allow a scrap of gratitude to enter in. In fact, it's our job to make sure the other person understands just how terribly they have hurt us. And if we hurt them in return, more's the better!

When, however, we loosen our grip on our interpretation of our feelings, seeing them as our idiosyncratic response, we can better allow the river of appreciation to flow between us, and the love that is available for us to experience is more easily accessed.

65

$\mathcal{I}$t's Positively Contagious

Blessed is the influence of one true, loving,
human soul on another.

—GEORGE ELIOT

I am a person who thrives in long-term relationships. I've been in three—one seven-year relationship, one fourteen-year, and my current one that is going on ten years. My first began when I was a freshman in college with a guy named Rick. Rick and I were the campus love story, but even we had our difficult moments and off days.

What I remember most about that aspect of our relationship is that I would get depressed and begin to talk to him about what I was upset about, which would bring him down so low that eventually we would both be absolutely flattened with misery and the sense that we could not possibly go on—together or apart. It was then, at the apex of misery, that I would think to myself, You better pull yourself out of this and cheer him up or you'll both sink forever. And so I would. I would focus on all that was still good—with us and with the world—and pretty soon we'd be laughing again.

Have you ever gotten into one of those vicious cycles with your partner? First one of you is annoyed or distant, and that sets the other one off, which only aggravates the first even more, which gets the other one more upset? Pretty soon, you are both spiraling down and away from one another, without any real idea of how it happened or what to do about it.

The reason this happens is that the two of you are a system, each having a profound effect on the other all the time. In a certain way, neither of you can do or say anything that is not having an effect on the other.

That's why, if you, all by yourself, begin to adopt an attitude of thankfulness toward your partner, your relationship will improve. It can't not. Your appreciation will have a positive effect, even if the other person is not consciously aware of your doing it. When you focus on the good in your mate and your relationship, you will be more loving, kind, sweet. That in turn will create the conditions in which he or she is more likely to be loving, kind, sweet. Which in turn will make you more appreciative of this wonderfully kind, sweet person sharing your life.

Theorists call this "positive contagion." We can—and do—catch wonderful things from one another, such as positivism and happiness, as well as negative things such as germs and disease.

You have a choice: Do you want to spread more joy in your love life or negativity? Happiness is contagious.

You'll Both Be Healthier

If fitness buffs spent just 10 percent of their weekly workout time—say twenty minutes a day—working on their marriages instead of their bodies, they would get three times the health benefits they derive from climbing the Stairmaster!

—JOHN GOTTMAN

Dave and Michelle are a young married couple I know who are very much in love. They glow with health and vitality. I've rarely seen either one of them sick. More than any other couple I know, they put their relationship front and center in their lives. "We even chose to work together," says Michelle, "so that we can spend more time together. We enjoy one another so much we are greedy about getting as many opportunities as possible."

So here is a question to ponder: Is there a relationship between their good health and their loving connection? The answer seems to be yes.

Recent research in marriage has revealed that those in a happy long-term marriage will live longer, healthier lives than either divorced people or unhappily married folks. Precisely why has not been fully understood, but some of the findings correlate strongly to similar findings on the health effects of positive attitudes: namely that by flooding the body with endorphins, both happy relationships and an attitude of gratitude promote lower blood pressure and heart rate, and boost immune function by increasing white blood cell and T-cell counts.

The effects are measurable: People in long-term happy relationships have less heart disease and suffer less from a variety of psychological ailments, including depression, anxiety, suicide, and substance abuse. It all adds up to a life expectancy that is four years longer, on average.

Add to that the research that has been done on the positive health effects of practicing gratitude, and you have compelling case for an attitude of gratitude in love. For example, a University of Pennsylvania study on heart transplant patients shows that those who practice appreciation felt better and had fewer ill effects one year after surgery than those who didn't. And a study at the HeartMath Institute demonstrates that thankfulness increases a person's parasympathetic activity, which lowers stress and blood pressure.

The most famous study was a longitudinal one on nuns. Researchers analyzed the journals of 180 nuns in their early twenties. Sixty years later, the researchers went back to the group. Those who were still alive tended to have been more thankful in their early journals!

As a society, we've become aware of the positive effects of proper exercise and diet on our health. But we still don't really understand or appreciate the positive effects on our physical well-being of practicing gratitude in our love lives. Nonetheless, as Gottman points out, we are profoundly influencing our health through the quality of the relationships we create.

This particular gift may not be as obvious as some of the others. But, speaking as someone who hates to work out, this is good news indeed—I would much rather offer appreciation to my husband daily than jog three miles, even if it didn't have health benefits. And, as an added bonus, it doesn't take as long either!

27

Conflicts Are Resolved More Easily

One kind word can warm three winter months.

—JAPANESE PROVERB

For most of my adult life, I thought fights between couples were supposed to be like high school debates. Each of us would marshal our arguments either for or against something, and it was my job to logically prove my position. If done properly, I believed, I would convince my mate that he was wrong and I was right, and then, gratefully seeing the errors of his ways, he would change. I spent a long time believing this, which contributed, among other things, to the death of my fourteen-year relationship.

Even after that loss, I still believed in my technique. (Slow learner on this score, I'm sorry to say.) Then I met Don. When, inevitably, we began to have disagreements, I trotted out my "I'm going to convince you I'm right by blasting you with just how wrong you are" method. But Don refused to do his part. "There is no way I can logically win an argument against you," he said one day, "and so I'm not going to even try." That stopped me cold in my verbal gymnast tracks. What the hell else to do? I have been exploring the answer to that question over the last ten years, and I continue to be a slow learner. But I *am* learning.

Studies on happy long-term relationships prove that conflict is inevitable. Two people, each with his or her own needs, wants, personal histories, and idiosyncrasies can't possibly come together without experiencing at least occasional friction. We will have disagreements, places in our lives that require negotiation. We will each need to compromise, to stretch and grow, to change.

This is not easy, at least for most human beings I know. We're comfortable the way we are, thank you very much. And so conflicts arise in which we each try to convince the other to see it our way.

What I've learned from recent research in conflict resolution is that there is virtually no way to convince someone to change some behavior unless we first make it clear that we fundamentally love and accept them for who they already are. If they (or we, for that matter) feel judged or misunderstood, there is no way they are going to be willing to be influenced in our direction.

A big light bulb went off over my head when I read this. All those years as the Debate Queen, as I judged and analyzed, I had been absolutely guaranteeing that my partner only become more defensive and en-trenched in the very behaviors that were upsetting me! What I should have done was to create the maximum possibility that my request for change would be heard through two practices of gratitude. First, to remember within myself all that I do appreciate about my spouse, so that I can take the second step in the heat of the moment—which is to offer the kind of genuine praise and appreciation that conveys that I fundamentally accept him for who he is. When I have been able to do this with Don, the results have been amazing. He is much more willing to see my point and adapt to my requests, and I have been much less of a harridan.

This has been an enormous gift in my life, and I hope it can be in yours. By employing the graciousness of gratitude, we will feel more willing to open our hearts to being influenced by the other, and find the solutions we need to break through impasses to a greater sense of connection.

31

ℛesentment Melts Away

Feeling resentful and used in our relationships plays havoc with our ability to be warm and loving.

—SUE PATTON THOELE

It was one of *those* days. You know, the ones where nothing, and I mean nothing, that the other person does is right, and you feel totally put upon. I had just returned from a full Saturday morning of errands and opened the door to a house that looked like a cyclone had descended. My interior monologue went something like this: "Don and Ana never lift a finger to clean anything. I have to do everything around here. Not only that, but they don't even appreciate any of my efforts because they trash the house as soon as possible and never utter a word of thanks for all I do. Why, oh why, do I have to live with such unappreciative slobs? I have been working like a dog and they don't even care. And where are they anyway? I'm going to give them a piece of my mind!" Angry? Resentful? You bet.

Then I noticed amid the clutter on the kitchen table a note from Don. It said that he had taken Ana out for the afternoon because he had noticed how hard I had been working and thought I could use a nap. Instantly my resentment dissolved in a wave of thankfulness: So he's a slob; at least he's a considerate slob.

That's one of the most amazing things about gratitude, I've found: It is virtually impossible to feel resentment at the same time. That's because resentment is negative case building: You always do this and you know I hate it . . . ; I'm always the one who has to . . . ; You never remember to . . . Resentment is a condition that's created by our paying attention to how much we've been used and put upon. Gratitude, on the other hand, is created by looking at how much we've been given. The two are mutually exclusive.

This gift of gratitude is no small thing. As Sue Thoele points out in her quote, resentment can really get in the way of our being loving. And if left to fester, it can destroy our relationship altogether.

This is not to minimize true inequities; some relationships are dangerously out of balance, with one person giving their all and the other just taking. I'm talking here about the ordinary, garden-variety relationship that is more or less a give and take. In these partnerships, resentment grows when we are solely focused on the take; practicing gratitude helps bring us into balance by reminding us about all that we have been given as well.

The More You're Thankful, the More You Receive

*Lately I've begun to notice that the more
I give thanks, the better my life goes. When I become
ungrateful, things tend to fall apart.*

—A COWORKER

Tina and John are friends of mine who have been to-gether for more than twenty-five years. They have a beautiful house and garden, and two incredible kids. They seem not only to care deeply for each other, but are extremely appreciative of one another. One day, I asked them where they got their attitude of gratitude.

"We weren't always like this," said Tina. "In fact, we seriously considered breaking up about ten years ago. But then we decided that we would be happier together than apart because each of us figured no one else would be able to put up with us. Essentially we chose to be happy with one another. And since that time, we mostly have been. And what's most amazing is that the more we appreciate each other and our lives, the more won-derful our life gets."

This is tricky territory. I don't mean to imply that if we are ungrateful we are necessarily punished with bad fortune. I know plenty of people who are not particularly grateful for their relationships but are loved nonetheless. I also know folks who do live in gratitude for their love who have been hurt greatly. Gratitude is not an insurance policy—it neither mandates that we get more goodies in the grab bag of life, nor protects us from the suffering that is inherent in being human. Gratitude is a feeling of fullness, a recognition of the heart of what we are receiving in this moment; it is not a wish or hope for the future.

However, I do believe that the more we offer our appreciation for what we have in our relationship, the more we are likely to get. That's because whatever we focus on tends to multiply: see misery everywhere and you'll get more miserable; feel thankful and receive more blessings.

Precisely why this is true is a deep mystery. One clue can be found in the new physics that seems to suggest that the very act of paying attention to something increases the possibility that it will continue to occur. In other words, the future is open—at least to some degree—to being influenced by our minds. As theorist David Cooperider puts it, and as I quoted in *Attitudes of Gratitude*, reality is "often profoundly created through our anticipatory images, values, plans, intentions, beliefs and the like."

In the context of gratitude in love, what this means is that the more we focus on the good, the more we create the possibility that our relationship will get better and better. And even if it has no effect on the future, noticing what's right in your love life sure helps you to feel better right this minute. And that's not bad either!

THE GIFTS OF
RELATIONSHIP
GRATITUDE

You'll Touch Love's Mystery and Majesty

The tender words we spoke to one another
Are stored in the secret heart of heaven
and one day, like rain,
they will fall and spread
And our mystery will grow green
all over the earth.

—RUMI

I am getting to the age where I have friends whose kids are getting married. One such young pair is Josh and Emily. It is always a joy for me to be around them because they are so obviously in love that they remind me to not take my husband for granted. They hold hands all the time, sit on one another's laps, call each other love names. When I am around them, soon I am sitting closer to Don, feeling warmer and cozier. That's because love begets love. The more any two of us create, the more we all bask in its glow.

Sages throughout time and of all religious persuasions tell us that in the end life all boils down to one question: Have we lived fully and loved well? The more that I study and practice gratitude, the more I believe it is one of the most powerful tools we have to be able to proudly answer that question.

Gratitude helps us live fully because it is the pause to notice what we are receiving, to register our fullness. And gratitude helps us love well by keeping us focused on the beauty in our relationship and the person we love.

When we practice gratitude in our intimate relationships, what we are really doing is making more love. We are taking what is already present and, by recognizing and valuing it, magnifying and intensifying it exponentially. This is a gift not only in our personal relationships, but in the wider world as well.

Rumi recognizes this in the poem quoted. He is saying that what we do privately, in the secrecy of our bedrooms as it were, contributes to the available reservoir of love in the world at large, and that in some unseen way, spreads over the Earth.

This is the realm of mystery, where words seem particularly inadequate. I don't know how it works exactly; I just trust that it does. I do know this: that the more I feel gratitude in my relationships, the more love I feel, and the more loving I am, not only to my husband, but to all those who cross my path. When I come to the end of my life, I want to be able to answer a resounding yes to the question of whether I have loved well, and so I will continue to practice.

MYTHS THAT
HOLD US BACK

It's the small things that are hard to do.
—JOHN B. FLANNAGAN

WHAT STANDS IN THE way of the easy flow of an attitude of gratitude in love? I've come to understand that the answer lies in a series of common viewpoints that prevent us from experiencing the miracle that thankfulness in relationships can bring. It is my hope that by looking at these myths deeply, we can begin to loosen their hold on us, freeing us up to make more joyful, relationship-affirming choices.

ℐ Need to Protect Myself

*Many of us spend our whole lives running from feeling
with the mistaken belief that you cannot bear the pain.
But you have already borne the pain. What you have not
done is feel all that you are beyond that pain.*

—BARTHOLOMEW

A male friend of mine, fifty-five years old, once told
me that his father has never said "I love you" to him
in his entire life. "I know he loves me," he said sorrow-
fully, "but he just can't say it. However, he's great at
pointing out all the ways I have screwed up and disap-
pointed him. I know he does care deeply for me, I wish
he would use the words at least once before he dies."

This man's father is by no means atypical. We all
hold ourselves back from experiencing the fullness of
love's joys; we just do it in different ways. Some of us
are stingy with our words; others with our bodies. Some
of us use anger to create distance; others stay busy, busy,
busy. Being discontent with the other is another great
method.

Why, when we all long for true connection, when
we spend a good deal of our lives searching for love, do
we set out to create as many barriers to it as we can

once we have it? One reason is that truly experiencing the depth of love that we could in our intimate relationships is plain scary. It sets off all kinds of fears. Some may be fears of being hurt like we were in childhood. Others are what therapists call "existential fears"—the fear that we will lose our identity if we merge with another being, that we will cease to exist as a self if we get too close to someone else. Yet another is that we will have to give up too much of our personal preferences and desires, our freedom to come and go as we want. And so to solve these dilemmas, which float below the surface of our awareness, influencing our behavior without our being conscious of them, we stay in a perpetual state of discontent. This dissatisfaction creates just enough distance for us to feel comfortable, like the man who loves his son but focuses on his failings so that he doesn't have to experience the magnitude of his love.

There is another, ultimately more satisfying, approach—to bring what is holding you back from a true appreciation and closeness to the one you love into the light of your awareness so that you can have more choice in the matter. Here's a way to begin. Complete the following sentences, adapted from *365 Days of Love* by Daphne Rose Kingma:

For me to be loved would be _____.

For me to know I am worthy of being loved would be _____.

For me to becoming more loving would require me to _____.

For me to be more appreciative to the one I love would be _____.

45

ℛelationships Are Hard

*Through patient observation, the law of nature becomes so
clear: whenever one generates mental negativity, one starts
suffering; and whenever one is free from negativity, one en-
joys peace and harmony.*

—S. N. GOENKA

Recently I was doing a radio program on gratitude
with an intelligent host who was well prepared and
asking me lots of good questions. I was trying to sound
erudite and expert, but realized that I was repeating myself: Gratitude is a matter of putting our attention on
what is right in our lives, and the more we do it, the
happier in love and life we will be. People should just
try it for themselves and see if it is true for them. When
I had said this in one way or another for perhaps the
third time, the host stopped and asked, "It can't be that
simple, can it?"

I believe the answer is yes. As I wrote in the intro-
duction, an attitude of gratitude is the most powerful
agent of relationship transformation I have ever experienced or heard of. It can be used anywhere, anytime, by
anyone. It requires no expenditure of money or even

time. You don't need to learn a three-step process or have relationship counseling to begin. All that's required is your willingness and the instant it takes in the moment to remember what you appreciate about the other person.

So if it is so easy, why don't we all do it all the time? I think there are a number of reasons, but the main one is this: We have been trained as a culture to focus on problems. In school, rather than getting our tests marked up 10 right, we're told we got 27 wrong. Rather than being supported in what we are good at, we are labeled as problems: learning disabled, ADD, hyperactive, depressed, overly right-brained, poorly coordinated, and so on. And the labels continue as adults: we're codependent, addicted to work, overly sensitive, introverted, an adult child of an alcoholic, suffer from low self esteem. . . . The list is endless. The consequence of all this labeling is, in the words of theorist Chris Argyris, that we become skilled in our own incompetence.

Naturally, therefore, when we get into a relationship, we tend to put all of our attention on its problems. That's what we do to ourselves, so that's what we do to our partner and the relationship itself. To support this negative view, a whole industry of books and relationship therapists have sprung up to theoretically address these problems. We are told that relationships are hard, they take lots of work, that men are from Mars and women are from Venus, and so of course it will be a struggle for the two to get along.

I am not trying to minimize the difficulties inherent in any relationship. Each relationship has its challenges, some more than others. What I am saying is that we've been trained to put all of our attention on that aspect rather than on the beauty that is also part of the equation. Awareness is like a flashlight that illuminates whatever it is shone upon. Shine it on what's wrong in your love life, and it will feel pretty bleak. Shine it on what's right, and you'll be basking in the glow of love. It really is that simple.

49

It's Dangerous to Be Too Happy

All that we can know about those we have loved and lost
is that they would wish us to remember them with more
intensified realization of their reality. What is essential
does not die, but clarifies. The highest tribute to
[what is lost] is not grief but gratitude.

—THORNTON WILDER

I was on the phone the other day working with a client. I asked her to name three things that she was totally content about in her relationship. "That makes me nervous," she replied. As we talked about her reaction, she realized that worrying about her husband and child made her feel as though she was protecting them, and if she stopped worrying, they would lose this protection. She knew rationally this wasn't true, and yet she could not shake the feeling.

As I have thought about what inhibits my own sense of gratitude and talked with other people, one issue comes up over and over: a magical belief that if we get too happy with our loves, they will be whisked away, whereas if we are in a state of discontent, we'll somehow preserve them. This seems to be so pervasive

51

that I hesitate to even call it a belief, for it seems to exist somehow as an embedded truth of our existence from which we operate: Get too happy and life will knock you down.

I've become fascinated with this phenomenon. Because obviously there is no one in the sky looking down and saying, "Hey, you there at 713 Lilac Street, you are too happy in your love. I'm going to bring you down a notch or two." No concept we have of God or the Divine includes that kind of pettiness.

So why do we *really* keep ourselves from feeling how appreciative we are that we are loved? Fear of loss, I believe. We've invented this piece of magical thinking to protect ourselves in advance from the pain we would feel were our relationships to end. Put another way, we are willing to sacrifice on a daily basis, year in and year out, experiencing the fullness of the love that is available at any given moment to stave off the potential of future pain.

Once I became aware I was doing this, I suddenly realized I had a choice: to continue to "protect" myself and cheat myself out of the maximum amount of joy I could have now, or feel the joy now and deal with the pain when and if it arrives. I choose joy now. Do I do it all the time? Of course not. But the more I do, the less I squander the love I can give and receive today.

There is no way to protect ourselves against loss, not really. We will lose everyone we've ever loved, at the moment of our death, if not before. But by appreciating what is in front of us as absolutely as much as we possibly can while we can, we redeem in advance the inevitability of loss.

It's Better to Be Right than Close

I'd rather die than give in.

—THE RYAN FAMILY MOTTO (HONEST)

I don't know about you, but when my husband and I have an argument, we can easily get into impasses that fundamentally come down to this:

"I want you to change your behavior."

"No, you're the one who should change."

"It's you who needs to change."

"No, I'm right and you're wrong. You need to change."

"No, you're the one who's wrong."

And so on, each of us unwilling to make the first move to transform the situation, each of us insisting that is the other person's responsibility to go first.

One of the amazing things about using gratitude to bring more joy and contentment into your relationship is that it is something you can do completely on your own. It doesn't require discussion or a joint commitment. The other person doesn't even need to know what you are doing. It is something you do in an instant by yourself, for your own good, the good of the other person, and the relationship itself.

Ah, but there's the challenge as well. Are you willing to be generously openhearted to this other person if he or she just goes on his or her merrily oblivious way?

It's my belief and experience that when one person opens their heart to the other, the dynamic between them inevitably changes for the better, but there is always that moment when you have to take the leap of faith and just do it, with no guarantees.

This can be difficult to do if we believe that a relationship is some kind of battle in which there are winners and losers, and that by God we're not going to be the one to give in first. When I am in this place, absolutely nothing will shake me. I am ready to fight to the death to prove I'm right.

But having fought to the death of one relationship, I've learned a couple things. One is that it always helps to remember what really matters. What do I really want? To be proven right or to have a loving relationship? (I've found it actually helps me to ask myself that specific question.) When I remember I want a loving relationship more than to have my petty ego satisfied, and that if I don't do something positive, I could destroy this relationship as I helped destroy the other, then it is possible for me to get off my high horse.

From level ground, I can see that if peace and love are the desired outcomes, it doesn't matter who "goes first." Or even if I am the only one to "do" it. If I just take a few breaths to remember why I love Don and our life together, my heart swells and the stalemate is over.

You too can do this, anytime, anyplace. All it takes is your willingness.

You Should Be Just Like Me

*When I walk on the beach to watch the sunset, I do not
call out, "A little more orange over to the right please,"
or "Would you mind giving us a little less purple in
the back?" No, I enjoy the always different sunsets as
they are. We do well to do the same with people we love.*

—CARL ROGERS

When I was first falling in love with Don, I loved
his loping walk, the fact that nothing could rattle
him. I loved his looking on the bright side, particularly
about the future. I loved his going with the flow, his appreciation of the moment as it unfolded rather than
being too focused on what he might accomplish. I loved
his goofy humor, his sense of playfulness. I loved his
focus on feelings and the heartfulness of any situation.
In a nutshell, I loved him because he was so different
from me. I moved fast, tended toward pessimism,
worked incredibly hard, was very serious, and had a
very mental approach to life.

After we had been together for a while and the endorphins had worn off, lo and behold, it was precisely
those things that I fell in love with in the first place that
now drove me absolutely crazy—he was so *slow*, he was

such a Pollyanna, he had no drive, he was not serious enough, he was so wrapped up in his feelings that he could not hold a rational conversation. In a nutshell, he was driving me absolutely crazy because he was so different from me.

Sound familiar? We fall in love with others for their uniqueness and spend most of the rest of our relationship trying to turn them into ourselves. What's *that* all about? I don't profess to have all the answers, but here's my thinking so far: We notice and fall in love with those differences because they represent the undeveloped aspects of ourselves. Then, once we are in the relationship itself, we are called upon to step up to the plate and grow. But there's a way we don't want to grow. We want to remain the same—it's easier, and we're used to it.

So in order to avoid having to change ourselves, we turn our attention toward changing the other person. After all, if he or she was just like me, then I wouldn't be shown on a daily basis what was missing in me. We'd just be two snug bugs in a rug of complacency.

Of course, the other person is busy trying to change us into them at the same time, and so this dynamic usually turns into a stalemate, which doesn't keep us from engaging in it ad nauseum. The problem with it is that it blinds us to the very qualities in the other that we fell in love with in the first place.

We can and do influence one another, but only to a certain degree. Don will always tend to look more on the bright side than I do, even though I practice it daily. I will always move faster and take action, even though he has speeded up somewhat. If I am so focused on turning him into me, I can't appreciate the fact that he is *not* me. And thank God he's not—or else we would never have a balanced checkbook, the garbage would never get taken out, and there would be no one at home to take care of our daughter as I go out to conquer the world.

61

If I Feel It, It's True

Your feelings aren't necessarily in line with reality. . . .
Honesty and truth are only identical in a fully
enlightened sage.

—BO LOZOFF

It was our first Christmas as a couple. I was eagerly awaiting what Don had chosen for me. Would it be jewelry? He has great taste and had given me several wonderful pairs of earrings. But it was in a rather large box, so I had my doubts. Opening the package, my jaw dropped, first in surprise and then in anger. It was an electric can opener. How could he give me such an awful present? Did he see me as his domestic slave? I was furious and let him know in no uncertain terms.

We live in an era that glorifies feelings. To a certain extent that is appropriate—in previous times, feelings were completely subjugated to duty, to survival, and we as a species are trying to come into some sort of balance.

Unfortunately, many of us have gotten out of balance the other direction. We now believe our feelings are paramount to anything and everything. If we feel angry, we should let it rip. If we feel withholding, then we should withhold. If we feel the other person is being a jerk, we should say so—or act as if we believe it. If we are afraid, then we shouldn't do whatever it is that is causing the fear. In this view of the world, our behavior follows our feelings. We feel a certain way and then behave accordingly.

I am no different. That was certainly how I lived most of my life, and, to some degree, still do.

But more and more, what I and others are discovering is that feelings are very transitory things, like clouds racing over a blue sky. Should we be basing behavior that can tremendously wound ourselves and others on such fast-moving phenomenon?

While our feelings are valid (i.e., they do exist), they may not be based on any solid truth. For instance, while I may feel that Don has intentionally wounded me by buying me a can opener, was hurting me his actual motivation? Most certainly not. But when I let my feelings have free rein in that situation, I made matters worse for him and me.

More and more, what I am coming to understand is that just because I feel something doesn't make it so. And in fact, many of my feelings are based on stories that I create about a situation. I chose to interpret the can opener as negative, saying to myself, "How unromantic," rather than saying, for instance, "How wonder-

ℱeelings Come before Behaviors

The Apostle Paul said, "Whatsoever things are pure or lovely or of good report, if there be any excellence in it, think on these things." Think on these things.

—MARY MANIN MORRISSEY

It was your average no-good, rotten day. I had spent sixteen hours getting home from a three-day trip to the East Coast, which involved getting up at 4 A.M., standing in long lines at airports, waiting for four hours crammed into a tiny seat on a crowded plane that couldn't take off until the fog lifted, and getting stuck in a massive traffic jam between the airport and home. When I opened the door to my house, I was not a happy camper—all I wanted was to crash, alone, in my bed. But Don and Ana Li had waited for me to have dinner, and Ana needed some mothering before bedtime.

As we sat down at the table, Ana reminded me that we needed to say "dinner words," which is our practice of each saying what we were thankful for that day. When my turn came, I struggled to think of anything positive to say. But then I realized that I was home, with two people who loved me and had even made me dinner.

How incredibly lucky I was! Flooded with love and thanks, I spoke my appreciation.

Before I began to practice gratitude, I used to think that I couldn't do it unless I *felt* grateful. I believed, as many of us do, that behavior follows feelings. Feel loving, act loving. Feel thankful, act thankful. Feel happy, act happy. And of course, it does work that way. Positive feelings do create positive actions. But because I didn't feel loving, happy, or grateful very often, I didn't act that way very often either. Which left me your average unhappy, ungrateful person.

Once I began to study happiness, I came to see that it works the other way as well, often more effectively. In other words, I could begin to feel loving by acting loving, feel grateful by choosing to focus on what I had to be thankful for. And the more I did that, the happier and more in love I felt.

The reason that's true is that, contrary to what I always believed, feelings can actually be created by the way we think (attitudes) and behave (actions). We don't have to wait for the positive feelings to descend. We can make them any time we want! The more I practice this, the more I experience how I can create positive feelings in myself (and others, by the way) by choosing to be grateful. You don't have to feel it to begin. All you have to do is begin, and the feelings will flow on their own.

$\mathcal{I}$t Has to Be a Certain Way

*An expectation, as they say, is a resentment
waiting to happen.*

—JON CARROLL

Jon Carroll writes for the *San Francisco Chronicle*. I always look at his column because I find him wise, and
wisdom is hard to come by these days, particularly in
the daily newspaper. Recently he became the grandfather of a one-year-old from China (a topic near and dear
to my heart, because my daughter is from there) and
wrote about meeting her for the first time. Here's a bit
of what he had to say: "I suspect I had expectations
about holding my grandchild for the first time. I believe
the expectations involved violins, bluebirds and baby
kisses raining on my face. When I held Lauren for the
first time, she took off my glasses, threw them on the
floor and demanded to be returned to Mommy."

Ah, expectations! They do have a way of forming,
but nothing is better at killing a sense of appreciation.
That's because, as Jon Carroll goes on to point out, they
quickly launch us into resentment when our expectations go unmet. It's hard to appreciate what is when we
are holding certain expectations of what should be:

What do you mean you don't run to the door and throw your arms around me when I come home from a trip but busily clean the house instead? What do you mean that your idea of a romantic Saturday night is to curl up together on the couch with a video? I expected dinner and dancing!

As human beings, we can't help but have expectations, which are stories about want we want and how we would like the other person to behave. There's nothing *de facto* wrong with that. It's fine to have preferences and wishes. However, expectations can really trip us up if we hold too firmly to them and allow them to get in the way of experiencing the love that is being offered in a form that we did not expect.

When we cling too tightly to our expectations of how it should be, we can easily overlook what is marvelous about what is. When we find ourselves in such a jam, the wise choice is to let go of what we expected and make ourselves available to what is being offered. That way, we don't allow resentment to grow.

In his column on his granddaughter, Jon Carroll writes about just such a choice. He realized that in order to love rather than resent his granddaughter, he had to put his expectations aside. In his words, he "recalibrated my dials and gauges." From there, he could begin to truly enjoy his granddaughter.

Where do you need to do a bit of recalibration? The woman that rushes around cleaning up for you may be expressing her love every bit as sincerely as if she threw her arms around you. The man who wants to curl up on the couch may be offering as much romance as the night on the town would give.

An attitude of gratitude in love asks that we let go of our fixed notions of how it all should be in order to experience the beauty of just how it is.

LOVE'S ATTITUDES
OF GRATITUDE

*The greatest discovery of my generation is
that a human being can alter their life by
altering their attitude of mind.*
—WILLIAM JAMES

ERE WE LOOK AT MENTAL outlooks that spawn a sense of gratitude for the one we love. Some may be natural to you or come easily; others may take a bit of practice. But all of them can be cultivated by anyone, anytime—it just takes a willingness to try. And the more we try, the more we will experience the maximum joyfulness available in our relationship.

You Can Choose What to Pay Attention To

Even a single moment of consciousness depends on so many factors, and when we change these various factors, the mind also changes. This is a simple truth about the nature of mind.

—HIS HOLINESS THE DALAI LAMA

A therapist friend once told me that the secret to working with someone as a client was to fall in love with them while you were together and then fall out of love with them when the time was up.

"How do you do that?" I wondered.

"It's easy," she said. "First I just focus on everything wonderful about them—for instance, their deep blue eyes, the way they care so much about their child, their sense of humor. Then to fall out of love, I pay attention to their flaws—their yellow teeth, their bad breath, how they get stuck in their lives. It works both ways."

We all have this capacity for selective attention and use it all the time, whether we are aware of it or not. We meet a new person—isn't she wonderful? She's so smart, so funny, so interesting. We become friends. After spending more time together, we begin to notice she's a bit of a drama queen—quite self-centered and prone to hypochondria. She hasn't changed. She had all those qualities, good and bad, when we met her. What's different is what we are choosing to pay attention to in her.

This capacity to choose goes to the heart of what an attitude of gratitude in love is all about. Our dear sweet mate, just like ourselves, is a blend of sterling and annoying qualities. When we fell in love, we noticed only the good. When we are annoyed or frustrated, angry or fed up, we notice only the bad. And because daily life gives us hundreds of opportunities to bump up against one another and rub one another the wrong way, gratitude helps us keep or regain our perspective that this is indeed a wonderful person we are sharing our life with.

When we recognize that we have a choice where to put our attention and that by choosing we can feel connected or disconnected, we realize in some deep way that we really have the power to be happy or discontent in love. Moment by moment, hour by hour, day by day, we are choosing whether to strengthen our love for this other person or our discontent. In this way, we really are creating our own reality.

We are each living in a relationship of our own making. Do you want yours to shine with the glow of thankfulness and joy or be tarnished by disgruntlement and frustration? You can, right now, choose to recall what is wonderful and let the glow warm you again.

It's Right to Notice What's Right

*The supreme happiness in life is the conviction
that we are loved.*

—VICTOR HUGO

I once heard a story about a teacher who was assigned to a class of childrn who were all very gifted according to a standardized test. And indeed they were incredibly talented, creative, and hardworking. They zoomed through the year and scored better on the end-of-the-year tests than any other class in the grade at that school. Then she discovered something—she had misinterpreted the scores at the beginning of the year; her class had been just average. Just average until she (accidentally) believed in them, which somehow helped them excel.

What was going on to produce such results? I believe it was that because this teacher was set up to see those kids as gifted, she spent all her time noticing how they were gifted and therefore supported them in doing their best. The reverse would have occurred if she had been told they were learning disabled—she would have spent her time noticing what was wrong and consequently helped them do worse.

This has profound implications for all sorts of things, including our relationships. Because we have all been trained to pay attention to what's wrong or broken in ourselves and others, we come to believe it's a smart thing to do. We may even go so far as to think (as I sometimes do) that I darn well better keep track of all the ways our spouse is screwing up because somehow that will keep us safe.

The truth is, however, we are living systems in the process of growing, and the natural way for us to grow is to track success, not failure. Innate learning is a process of trial and error, in which error is immediately discarded. When a baby learns to drink from a cup, she first tries and misses, getting cereal. She tries again and gets Mama's hair. She tries again, and gets cup. Hair, cereal, cup. Hair, cup. Soon it's cup. Cup. Cup. To learn, the baby didn't beat herself up for getting hair or cereal. If she did, she probably would never learn. She just uses the information from each try to improve her performance, tracking what worked and letting go of what didn't.

Unfortunately, by the time we're adults, we've had our natural system of tracking what's right in any given situation so messed with that it's hard to believe it could possibly be effective in our love lives. But the truth is, the more we notice what's right, the more we will go toward the light of that rightness, individually and together.

Noticing what's right reminds us of where we want to be in our relationship and the resources available to us to get there. It frees up the energy we've got currently tied up in anger or blame or guilt to find positive solutions and feel a greater sense of connection. Once again we experience the greatest feeling in the world—that we are loved by someone wonderful!

Receptivity Is Key

Gratitude is an act of grace, a way of blessing yourself into a future abundance of gifts. For when we are grateful we open a channel of receiving in ourselves.

—DAPHNE ROSE KINGMA

I was sitting at the computer writing this book on a Sunday morning. Don and Ana Li were in the garden. Ana was supposed to be not "bothering" me. In she snuck, very quietly, with a bunch of flowers in her hand. "Look at these, Mama. I picked them for you."

As I got up to find a vase, two thoughts vied for my attention—the first, that I would never finish this book if she kept interrupting me; the second, that she was so cute and sweet that it didn't matter. Then I took a moment to really look at the flowers in my hand. She had put together a combination of purple, pink, and red that was truly stunning.

Suddenly I was flooded with thankfulness—for my husband who grew the flowers, for my daughter who could put them together, for the flowers themselves for such a source of beauty, for a Sunday morning that could contain such a gift, for the fact that I was alive to receive the gift, for my eyes that could perceive it all.

Gratitude is a feeling that is created when we become aware of what we are receiving. We may have been receiving it all along, but it is only when we become aware of what we have that we experience a sense of thankfulness.

Like me with Ana's bouquet, in order to have the experience, we need to open our hearts and actually take in what we are receiving. I call that "capacity receptivity." Without receptivity, we are like the hungry ghosts of the Buddhist hell realms. Hungry ghosts are beings that are always starving even in the midst of plenty because their throats are so small the food can't get down to fill their huge bellies. So they roam, perpetually hungry, perpetually unsatisfied because they can't take in what is right in front of them. Sound like anyone you know?

Receptivity is the antidote to the hungry ghost phenomenon—the ability to open our hearts wide enough to take in what is available to us. We each receive great gifts every day. But without receptivity, we simply don't notice, we can't feel what we are getting.

Receptivity is an attitude that we choose—to allow life to enter us, move us, transform us. It is enhanced by practices—for instance, of consciously taking in the world around you through your eyes, ears, and body—and by taking time. It's hard to be receptive when you are going ninety miles an hour.

Take a moment to try it now. Think of one good thing your mate has done for you in the last week. Really allow yourself to receive the gift that was given. How do you feel now?

$\mathscr{I}$t's Not about Being a Doormat

You can't say yes if you can't say no.
—Dawna Markova

My husband Don smoked pot every day for seventeen years. When I met him, he had quit six weeks earlier. While he swore he would never do it again, I naturally was very concerned. I knew that, given my family history, it was absolutely unacceptable to me to be involved with an active addict. I made it very clear that if he were to begin again, I would leave him. He, on the other hand, made it clear that, given his family history of physical abuse, he would leave me if I ever hit him. We reiterated those limits when we married three years later. I am happy to report that we've been together now for ten years, and he's never gotten stoned again and I've never hit anyone.

I tell this story because it is crucially important to understand that there are relationship situations that are purely unacceptable and should not be tolerated. Practicing gratitude in love is not about putting up with anything. It's not an excuse for you to avoid terrible problems—his alcoholism, her spendthrift ways, his physical abuse, her affairs.

I do not want in any way, shape, or form to be seen as advocating the practice of gratitude in relationships as a form of denial or as a way to set yourself up for abuse. Sometimes it is not right to look at what's right. Sometimes what's right is to assess the situation with a cold clear-headedness and get the hell out.

In order to truly practice gratitude in love, we have to know where our limits are, what is unacceptable for us. Otherwise, we can become doormats, putting up with any reprehensible behavior because we are "focusing on what's still good." Sometimes for our own good and the good of our family, we must turn our attention to the negative behavior and set a boundary—beyond this I will not go or, as a Norwegian saying a friend recently told me goes, "Up with this I will not put."

The problem for many of us is not in this arena, however. We jump to the negative at the drop of the proverbial hat—the fact that he promised to take the trash out and forgot, or she lost her car keys for the twentieth time this week—and lose all perspective of the larger picture of love. That's where an attitude of gratitude comes in very handy.

But in order to give yourself over fully to cultivating such an attitude, it is crucial that you know when *not* to do it as well. What behaviors in your intimate relationship would be unacceptable to you—deal breakers, as it were? The more we know where our limits are, the more we can foster openheartedness within them.

$\mathcal{A}$ssume the Best

We must beware of committing the fatally common
fallacy of assuming that all we see is all there is to see.

—C. W. LEADBETTER

I have a friend I've known for twenty years. For the first ten of those years, I never heard her say one good thing about her husband. From her point of view, he was self-absorbed, coldhearted, and completely unsupportive. From my point of view, he was a nice guy who went out of his way to please her—they moved several times because she wanted to, he was a loving stepfather to her children, and he supported her desire to be an artist without making any demands on her to contribute financially to their life. Given that you never know what goes on inside a relationship, I always figured that the truth was somewhere in between our two perspectives.

Finally they divorced. She and I still see one another now and then, and she is no happier. In fact, she's still complaining about him ten years after the breakup.

In one of the most amazing studies I have heard of regarding the relationship between focusing on what's right and relationship happiness, researchers found that couples who said they were happily married noticed virtually all the positive things their partners did, while unhappy couples underestimated their spouses' loving intentions and actions by *50 percent!* And this was not a self-report—researchers actually tracked the actions of each couple objectively while asking each partner to note the actions as well, and then compared the lists. What amazingly powerful confirmation that our attitudes really do shape our reality.

Now that I've read about this study, I'm convinced that my friend really didn't see what her husband was giving her. For whatever reasons, she was totally blind to his positive actions, and as a consequence, in a certain way, she never did receive his love. His financial support, his parenting, his willingness to move over and over again never even registered on her internal radar screen.

What this means is that when we get stuck in a rut of negativity about our mate, all the loving things that he or she is actually doing may be invisible to us. In a terrible self-fulfilling prophecy, by assuming the worst about the other person, we make it so by under-noticing the good. Conversely, when we assume the best, our eyes are open to all that we are being given, and therefore we are able to receive it.

Don't you want to maximize the possibility that you

actually register what you are receiving? If so, assume the best about your partner. Otherwise you may end up like my friend—throwing away something of value because you have deemed it worthless.

You're Not Perfect Either

The bottom line is that (a) people are never perfect,
but love can be, (b) that is the one and only way that
the mediocre and vile can be transformed, and (c) doing
that makes it that. We waste time looking for the perfect
lover, instead of creating the perfect love.

—TOM ROBBINS

I don't know about you, but when my husband does
something to irritate me, it is easy for me to go off on
a trip in my mind about just how flawed a human being
he is. Full of annoying habits and seemingly silly strug-
gles. As compared to me, of course, who is much more
highly evolved. Come to think of it, I surely deserve
someone much better than him—someone richer, more
successful, more intellectual, more spiritual. . . .

Ah, ego. How easy it is, at least for me, to inflate my
wonderfulness and deflate his. My faults are minor
things that any loving mate should easily overlook, if
they are noticed at all; his are Grand Canyon issues that
might just be relationship breakers.

Sound familiar? We usually are more willing to give
ourselves the benefit of the doubt than we are the other
person. After all, we understand just how hard we are

trying. The other person, on the other hand, is not only not perfect, but perhaps should be traded in for a better model.

When I get into a place like this, it helps to take myself in hand and say, Listen honey, you are not perfect either. You have plenty of foibles, and anyone else you could possibly find would too. After the first glow of love faded, he would annoy you just as much, if not more. So get off your high horse and remember what there is to appreciate in the person right in front of you. Just as you want him to ignore your flaws and focus on what's wonderful about you, he wants that from you.

When we remember that we are as much of a mixed bag as the person we love, our hearts are filled with gratitude that we are loved, despite our imperfection. And that in turn allows us to reach out once again with an open heart.

96

The Other Person's Quirks Are Delightful

Appreciation is a wonderful thing: It makes what
is excellent in others belong to us as well.

—Voltaire

George and Grace have been together for thirty years, longer than any of my other contemporaries. So I've always been curious about what makes their relationship work. From what I've observed and what they say, I've concluded that the secret to their happiness is that they have truly found a way to appreciate the quirks in one another's personalities rather than being driven crazy by them.

"George is a great putterer," says Grace. "He putters in the garden, he putters around the house. It is impossible to get him to move quickly. It used to drive me insane, but about fifteen years ago, I realized that we were headed for divorce if I couldn't make my peace with this. It was only after I began to study meditation that I realized that George naturally has the equanimity people meditate decades for. So now when I see him puttering around, I just call him my live-in Buddha."

George does a similar thing with Grace. "Grace is always going on in a heated fashion about one thing or another. I used to try to get her to calm down, but that was totally ineffective. Finally I got it that what I am attracted to in her is her passion for life. Now when she gets worked up about something or other, in my mind I just think, 'That's my firecracker going off again' and I smile."

Grace and George know a lot about an attitude of gratitude in love. They know that one of the great relationship challenges each of us faces is to find the jewel in the irritating, annoying, or downright upsetting things the other person does. We can ask them to change, beg them to change, pray for them to change, and they might—somewhat. But when it comes right down to it, we have to make our peace with the foibles of one another.

But what Grace and George have done goes beyond that. They haven't just reconciled themselves to each other's quirks. They have figured out a way to find them charming. And that is truly wonderful. Because the more we can appreciate these quirks in one another, the more ground of positive regard we create together.

How can you find delight in the little irritating habits or personality tics in the person you love? One place to begin is to consider that perhaps what annoys you in the other is something you need to learn for yourself. For instance, I am often exasperated by Don's slowness. But guess what I have trouble doing? Slowing down. The more I can see it as something I need, the more I can appreciate him for it.

LOVE'S
ATTITUDE OF
GRATITUDE

ℒove Is Truly a Gift

*Love has no other desire but to fulfill itself. To melt
and be like a running brook that sings its melody
to the night. To wake at dawn with a winged heart
and give thanks for another day of loving.*

—KAHLIL GIBRAN

Recently I had lunch with a wonderful woman. She's
sensitive, attractive, smart, and funny. The word I
think most often of in her presence is *lovely*. She's also
alone and has been for many years now. Her lack of an
intimate relationship saddens her deeply. At lunch she
spoke of her longing for love, and my heart just broke
for her. Of anyone I have ever known, she certainly "deserves" to be loved. And yet, she is alone.

Sometimes when I am really stuck in the pit of negativity about my relationship, what helps most is to remember what a privilege it is to be loved at all. What a
miracle to be blessed by the grace of another person's
presence, attention, care. So many wonderful people I
know are alone, longing for just this very experience that
I am now mentally relegating to the garbage heap. How
many women friends have cried on my shoulder over

their lack of a special someone to share their lives with? How dare I take it for granted or, worse, denigrate it!

Being loved is a privilege not to be scoffed at. It is a great and powerful mystery that one person loves another. In some way, it has nothing to do with us personally, for thousands, if not millions, of equally worthy people stand outside the experience wistfully looking in. It is a gift of the universe not to be taken lightly.

The same is true for the opportunity to love another human being. What a chance to practice patience, flexibility, constancy, commitment. What an occasion for soulmaking—to learn to see someone for who they really are rather than a reflection of who you would wish them to be, and to want the highest good for that being, regardless of your own self-interest.

When we remember what a tremendous gift we have been given in the opportunity to love and be loved, we can't help but feel a swell of appreciation for the possibility itself.

You Are a Great Gift Too

Don't forget to love yourself.

—SØREN KIERKEGAARD

A woman I know is married to a man who really loves her. It's quite obvious from the outside. But she's always complaining to me that he doesn't love her, and nothing he does, and nothing I try to help her see, will convince her otherwise. Because I've gotten nowhere with her, I've become intrigued with why she is so stuck.

I came to see that the problem is that she doesn't really love herself, and so she can't believe that anyone else loves her either. She keeps trying to get him to fix the problem by proving once and for all that he does love her, but it can't work. What she needs to do is love herself, and then she'll see the love that's already coming from him.

When it comes to spreading around gratitude in your relationship, don't forget yourself. You deserve your loving regard as much as your mate does. You too are full of remarkable qualities, you too have been loving when times got tough, you too have been giving when you didn't feel like it.

If we focus solely on the other person, we can get out of balance, feeling unworthy of the love that is pouring from our partner to us because we don't think we have anything to offer in return, or, as in the case of the woman I know, not feeling the love that is there. This is a particular trap for women, who tend toward low self-esteem (although men can have it too).

Low self-esteem creates a feeling of unworthiness in which you become blind to all that you are giving and doing, and over-inflate what the other person is contributing. This is a spiritual emergency, because in this state you've lost touch with the beauty of your essence. From this place we can neither be grateful to ourselves or, really, to the other person. For our systems then try to rectify the situation, to bring us back into balance, by deflating the other person in our minds so that we don't have to feel badly that they love us.

It is a wondrous miracle that this other person loves you. But it is equally wonderful that you, a magnificent, unique human being, love him or her. There has never been one such as you, and there never will be again. You have so much to offer in love.

When you remember that you are a gift too, you can be grateful to yourself—for your capacity to love, for the work you do on your relationship's behalf—and take

an equal place at love's table, neither above nor below
the person who shares your life.

LOVE'S
ATTITUDE OF
GRATITUDE

ⳍwareness without Judgment Creates Change

There's no word in Tibetan for "guilty." The closest thing is 'intelligent regret that decides to do things differently.'

—GESHE MICHAEL ROACH

I've been working as a thinking partner/coach with people all over the country the last couple of years. Individuals who want to create intentional change and seek some support in doing that. And so I've had the incredible privilege of accompanying people as they make conscious changes in their lives. What I have noticed, over and over again, is that the most powerful vehicle for transformation is awareness without judgment.

What I mean by that is telling ourselves the truth about current reality without guilt-tripping or shaming ourselves or blaming someone or something else: I said I was going to take a walk around the lake every day, and I only did it three times in a week. Isn't that interesting? I wonder how well I will do this coming week. Or, I spend forty-five out of every sixty waking minutes worrying about money. Isn't that interesting? I wonder what that is about? What I have observed is that the more people can become aware without judgment, the more they change in the direction they desire.

The "Isn't that interesting" part is crucial, because it creates a mood of curiosity, and curiosity and judgment are mutually exclusive mindsets—one is a state of wonder, the other is a verdict where someone or something has to be held accountable. Guilt, blame, shame all get in our way when we want to create change, because they are such bad feelings that we want to run from whatever is making us feel that way and so make no progress at all.

The other good thing about awareness without judgment is that it creates a blank slate for tomorrow, where you just pick yourself up and try again, no guilt or shame to overcome, no time wasted finding someone else to blame. You just decide to try again the next day or the next minute.

So, without blame, shame, or guilt, take a moment to reflect on how much time in a day you spend appreciating your loved one and your relationship, and how much of your mental time goes into thinking to yourself or complaining out loud. Tell yourself the truth and say, "Isn't that interesting." Then, if it is your intention to spend more time in appreciation than complaint, tell yourself that you can begin again right now.

It doesn't matter how many months or years you've focused on the negative. You can always begin again. But no matter what, please treat what you discover with mercy and compassion by invoking those three little words: "Isn't that interesting."

$\mathcal{L}$ove Is the Cauldron in Which Our Souls Are Tempered

Through our beloved we are once again brought face to face with what is unresolved in us. We meet again our father's absence or our brother's envy, our mother's cruelty or our sister's competition. We see our own childhood mirrored in every direction. Though love we are invited to reenter them again but differently, to reexperience and grieve the losses of the past, and thus to redeem them.

—DAPHNE ROSE KINGMA

M y father was a small-town doctor who worked six days a week, twelve to eighteen hours a day. Naturally I did not see him often. I loved him very much, though, and it can fairly be said that aside from going to school, my life was spent waiting for my father to come home and pay attention to me.

When I became an adult, I fell in love with Will, a man who in many ways was like my father—intelligent, articulate, and hardworking. But there was one crucial difference—he was with me all the time, for we worked together at the same weekly newspaper. Soon, however, things changed—suddenly he was gone just like my father, and I was sitting around pining, just as I had done as a child.

Whether or not I chose this situation to face that childhood wound is not important here. What does feel significant is that through this difficult relationship dynamic, I was given an opportunity to face my early loss, feel it, and transform it. I remember being on the phone once complaining to my friend Daphne that it was no different than my childhood. She stopped me and said, "No, this time you have the right to complain." I must say, that *did* feel good. And I remember clearly a time when Will said to me over the phone from a far distance, "If you really need me, I will get on a plane right now and come home." My father never said that!

What does this have to do with an attitude of gratitude in love? Well, the more we can see our relationships from this higher plane—that in some senses they are vehicles for our own emotional healing and psychological transformation—we can stop expecting them to be a nonstop joy ride in which we just get to coast in our lives.

Several times in the early years of our being together, when, through our relationship, Don was facing a lot of muck from the past, he would moan, "Why does it have to be so hard? I thought if I just fell in love, everything would be fine." Wrong.

If we fully embrace the truth of what we are doing in our relationships with one another—healing and growing our psyches and souls, which entails pain as well as beauty—then something miraculous happens. We become grateful for the opportunity the relationship is offering us to heal. We actually become thankful for the painfully repetitious dynamic, because through it we somehow change.

The change doesn't come easily or necessarily in the form we imagined. For me about my father, it entailed stopping waiting for the man in my life to come home and instead developing the masculine part of myself that went out in the world to make something manifest. But I would never have done that if Will hadn't been gone all the time and if, ultimately, he hadn't left me. And for that I am grateful.

It's All about Learning

*I came to the conclusion that the human race is not divided
into two opposing camps of good and evil. It is made up
of those who are capable of learning and those who are
incapable of doing so. . . learning as the process of absorbing
those lessons of life that enable us to increase peace and
happiness in our world.*

—NOBEL PEACE PRIZE-WINNER AUNG SAN SUU KYI,
ON WHAT SHE LEARNED FROM SIX YEARS
OF HOUSE ARREST IN BURMA

My husband Don was never in a relationship longer than nine months before he met me at age thirty-six, although he always wanted to be, and was often alone for long stretches of time. Once I asked him whether he had fallen into despair at any point during those years. "No," he said, "when an relationship would end, I would be grateful for what I'd learned and think to myself that I had more to learn before I could be in a long-term relationship." (Now you see some of why I love him.)

That's what a true attitude of gratitude is all about: seeing our relationships as opportunities to learn more about how to love and therefore being grateful for all the lessons learned, even the painful ones.

It's human nature to want to pick and choose—to prefer comfort over discomfort, ease over difficulty. It's easy to be grateful for the wonderful things that the other person gives us—the bouquet of flowers, the home-cooked meals, a warm body to snuggle against on cold evenings. It's much harder to be grateful for the challenging things—for the bullying that taught us to stand up for ourselves, for the kitchen messes that taught us to be more tolerant, for the arguments that taught us how to express our anger in more constructive ways.

When we see learning as the goal, it is much easy to accept and appreciate the more difficult lessons. For no learning happens inside our comfort zone—we do what we've always done and get the results we always got; that's why it feels comfortable. True learning happens outside the comfort zone—when we are stretched beyond our current definitions of ourselves and forced to try something new. Aung San Suu Kyi did not choose to be imprisoned in her house for six years; she wasn't even allowed to leave to say good-bye to her husband dying in England. But she still maintains it was an invaluable learning experience.

Most of us are luckier than Aung San Suu Kyi. We have chosen the relationship we are in; we are not imprisoned. And yet there will be much that happens within the container of our relationship that will not be of our choosing. When we hold that it's all about learning, we can resist less and appreciate more even the difficult lessons.

LOVE'S
ATTITUDE OF
GRATITUDE

We're Here to Bring More Love into the World

The goal of our life should not be to find joy in marriage,
but to bring more love and truth into the world.
We marry to assist one another in this task.

—LEO TOLSTOY

One of the things I do in the world is help lead retreats on personal renewal for corporate executives at Robert Redford's resort at Sundance, Utah. It's a chance for people in transition to reflect on what really matters to them as they contemplate their next steps. Often attendees bring their significant others, and occasionally I am touched by the deep love that is evident between a couple. I remember one woman in particular saying to me of her ten-year relationship, "My relationship is the most important thing to me. I found love relatively late in life and so being with [her partner] is my number one priority." What a joy to see such sustained enjoyment and commitment.

That's why I love this quote by Tolstoy. It reminds me that a relationship isn't just about the emotional and spiritual growth of the two individuals within it, but a vehicle by which more love gets created in the world at large. When we see our relationship as this higher calling, we see that it is about more than two people getting their individual needs met, but a sacred container that affects everyone who ventures into its orbit. If we love one another well, and focus on the ways we do that, we not only create our own happiness, but we provide a model for our children, our friends, our community. The holiness of the task—to collectively and individually bring love and truth into the world—gives a weight to what we are doing that is appropriately heavy.

Thinking about a relationship in this way helps me remember not only to be grateful to Don, my partner in love, but to the relationship itself. Of course I could offer love to the world on my own, and I do that. So does he. But together we do, too, multiplying our efforts. How wonderful!

THE PRACTICE OF GRATITUDE IN LOVE

Like a wish or a work of art, the beauty of love is sculpted over time. The love you imagine and desire will become yours only through a constancy of effort.

—DAPHNE ROSE KINGMA

ERE'S WHERE WE MOVE into action, taking all the knowledge we've gained so far and putting it into practice. This is where we prove our mettle as loving partners, for while it may be easy to understand the ideas behind the practice of gratitude, actually doing it is how we truly grow. By applying ourselves, we go beyond book learning to an embodied wisdom, as we learn to "practice what we preach."

In order to do these practices, it's important to differentiate between a person and his or her behavior. Someone can do something that makes us furious or sorrowful—that's behavior—and we can still love him

or her as a human being. When we differentiate between behavior and the person, we understand that
finding things we cherish about him or her does not
mean we condone their negative behavior. This allows
us to feel free to practice gratitude without thinking it
requires us to put up with anything.

123

Just Begin

People deal too much with the negative,
with what is wrong. . . .Why not try and see positive things,
to just touch those things and make them bloom?

—THICH NHAT HANH

As I speak about gratitude on the radio and TV, and at speeches, people always ask me, "How do I start?" And more and more what I find myself saying is, "Just begin."

That's all it takes—begin to look at what is positive about your relationship and the person you are sharing it with. It doesn't require anything fancy or complicated. You don't have to keep a gratitude journal, although that may be useful for some folks. You don't need to think of fifty things you are thankful for before you go to sleep every night. All you need to do is to begin to notice what's good about your love life.

But for some of us, it is hard to look at the positive because we've trained so long and well at looking at the negative, so I will suggest a daily practice. Sometimes when we want to learn a new behavior, it helps to put a bit of structure around it, as long as the structure is not so cumbersome that it becomes too much work.

Recent research confirms the power of this daily approach. In a study done at the University of California-Davis, subjects got more benefits from writing daily in a gratitude journal than those who wrote only weekly.

Here's a daily practice that has worked for me. At dinner (Don and I almost always have dinner together unless I am away for work; if you don't, pick another time, like bedtime or first thing in the morning), take turns saying one thing you are thankful for about the other person that day. That's it.

This practice has really helped Don and me when we are feeling disconnected because it forces us to think of one good thing, even if we don't feel like it. And it asks that both of us think of something, which helps the two of us create an asset focus. When I am away from Don, I do it on my own. As I am falling asleep, I simply think about what I appreciate about him.

This is great for preventing that dread relationship disease—Taking the Other Person for Granted. So begin today with just one thing you are each thankful for.

ℬe Explicit

Don't be cool, reserved, judicious about expressing
your love and gratitude. Be effusive. Give details. Waste it.
Where there is the smallest fraction, share it.

—JOHN MACENULTY

When I look back on my fourteen-year relationship, I see that it faltered and failed for many reasons. But one of the main ones was that both of us were
terrible ingrates toward one another. Each of us gave so
much—I helped him raise two small children, he financially and emotionally supported me in my career—but
neither of us thanked one another very often for those
gifts. As a consequence, we both ended up feeling bit-
ter. The more each of us felt resentful, the less appreciative we felt, and the less appreciative we were, the more
we felt resentful. It was a vicious cycle.

Just as there are vicious cycles, so can there be up-
lifting ones. The more appreciation we can give to one
another, the more we will *want* to give, and the greater
an abundance of love we will create.

There is an art to giving appreciation. Sometimes a
simple "Thank you" will suffice (and it is certainly better than nothing). But what truly creates the circle of

abundant lovingness is specific, believable, and true praise. Too general and it is meaningless; too over-wrought and it won't feel sincere.

For instance, there is a world of difference between, "Thanks for taking out the garbage," and "You are so steadfast in taking out the garbage every week. I really appreciate it." The first, while nice, compliments the action. The second reveals to your sweetheart a facet of his or her character that you are thankful for. In a way, it exposes the deeper meaning behind the action, so that the doer gets a clearer picture of him or herself.

In this way, our thanks itself becomes a gift. When we are effusive and explicit with our acknowledgment, not only does our partner experience our love, but our thanks becomes a mirror that enables our mate to know him or herself more deeply.

Try it for yourself. For three days, consciously go out of your way to explicitly thank your partner for what he or she does for you. What precisely are you thankful for? When she balances the checkbook, is it her finesse with money so you don't have to worry about that part of your life? When he offers a joke, is it that his lighthearted-edness buoys you up in hard times? The more precise you can be in your communication, the better.

Notice what effect it has on you and your relation-ship when you offer specific praise.

Practice Truly Seeing

Seeing takes time.
—GEORGIA O'KEEFFE

What's the difference between when we first fell in love and now? Mostly it's that when we were falling in love, we spent a long time mooning over one another. Noticing how he crosses his feet just so, how she has a little mole by the side of her mouth. As time goes on, those traits are still there, but we've gotten so used to them that we don't even notice them any more.

That's sad. Because the beauty of those traits are still available for us to be touched by, again and again. It just takes noticing. Seeing as if for the first time all the splendor in the other.

When our relationship is new, we don't need a special practice to do this—it just happens automatically.

When we've been together for a while, however, our eyes tend to glaze over and the miracle of the human being right in front of our noses is less obvious. But we can recapture that sense of awe and fall in love all over again, simply by paying attention. My friend Dawna calls this "the thermostat of love"—we can turn it on and off by choosing what to pay attention to.

One way to turn up the heat on your love is through Best Friends Night. For a month, agree to spend an evening a week together, just the two of you. The point of Best Friends Night is a chance to acknowledge the great things about your mate. You can sit side by side, back to back, go for a walk and talk, or write notes to one another. The point is to acknowledge to the other person the difference he or she's made in your life and all the things you love about your partner.

When one of you is doing the acknowledging, the other just listens without saying anything. That's the tricky part. It's easy for many of us to brush off acknowledgment or appreciation. Silence makes it more difficult to flick off. Then you switch, and the other person tells you why you matter so much to them. At the end of the month, decide if you want to do this regularly.

Attitudes of
gratitude
in LOVE

Make a Gratitude Laundry List

How do I love thee?
Let me count the ways.
—ROBERT BROWNING

I have a confession to make. In fights with Don, I have a tendency to do something all relationship experts caution against: rather than sticking to the specifics at hand, I wander through my mind remembering every time he did or said anything remotely related so I can build a more effective case for his terribleness. (I know, I know—it's not good. I've gotten better about it.)

One of the things such behavior indicates is that somewhere in my memory banks is a laundry list entitled Every Bad Thing Don Has Done. It sits there, waiting for me to call it up in times of perceived need.

Realizing this, I also realized something else, which is quite embarrassing. I don't have an equivalent Gratitude Laundry List just sitting there waiting to be accessed. Why not? He has done innumerable charming, loving, and wonderful things for me. Realistically, they far outweigh the negatives. But somehow the list of negatives seem like a safety blanket—as long as I keep track of how I have been injured it won't happen to me again—whereas the positives are momentary feel-good things not worthy of paying lasting attention to.

The more I understand what the practice of gratitude can do to keep love alive, the more I understand the faultiness of my thinking. I should be engraving all the good deeds, qualities, and moments in gold, and discarding the fights, the frustrations. The more I remember what's wonderful, the more loving I feel and the more openhearted I am.

The good news is that if I can keep a list of the negatives, I certainly can also keep a positive one handy too. And so can you.

Try it right now. You can make a written list or create one in your mind. Why do you love your mate? What wonderful things have they done for you in your time together?

Make your list long and engrave it somewhere. Then when times are tough and you've lost your perspective, you can bring it out and make a case for why it's worth going on.

ⅅo It on Your Own

To love is not a passive thing. To love is active voice.
When I love I do something, I function, I give.
I do not love in order that I may be loved back again,
but for the creative joy of loving. And every time I do so love
I am freed, at least a little, by the outgoing of love, from
enslavement to that most intolerable of masters, myself.

—BERNARD IDDINGS BELL

I don't know about you but I am glad that my sweetheart is not a mind reader. Because I am pretty convinced our relationship would never have lasted if he
could hear my uncensored thoughts twenty-four hours a
day. That's because I have a very strong judgmental
mindset. My mind has been trained from birth to notice
what, in my humble opinion, is wrong with everyone
and everything, and then to try and fix it.

This actually is a thinking strength, identified by the
Gallup Organization in their book *Now Discover Your
Strengths*, as "restoration," or the desire to fix things. And
I *am* good at finding solutions when someone presents
me with a problem; the trouble comes in because I can't
turn it off—I judge myself and others (particularly my
special other) all the time, at least internally. Perhaps

that's why I got so interested in the practice of gratitude—it gives that part of my mind something more positive to do, that is, to focus on all that is whole, rather than just on what is broken. Nonetheless, it does mean that I spend a lot of time having critical judgmental thoughts.

If this is something that you struggle with as well, the good news is that your partner is *not* psychic and that you can actually use those negative thoughts as a trigger to think of something positive.

Here's how it works: Take notice of how often in a day you think something judgmental or critical of your mate. Then, at some other point in the day when you are not angry or upset, think to yourself an equal number of things that you appreciate about him or her and that you would never want to change. For instance, if you wish he would finally learn to pick up his clothes from the floor, later you might recall his love of nature and how you would not want to change that for the world. The task is, for everything you wish were different, you remember something that you would never want to be different.

The best thing about this practice is that it all takes place in you—the other person doesn't have to even be aware that you have thought something negative or

Attitudes of gratitude in LOVE

worked on looking for what you can appreciate. All he or she knows is that you are more loving!

Try it next time you find yourself annoyed or judgmental, and notice what effect it has on you and your relationship. You may not be able to stop the critical thoughts, but you may be able to counterbalance them so that the love will continue to flow between you.

Celebrate Your "Usness"

The third body is like an invisible glue
that holds you in union.

—CONNIE ZWEIG AND NEIL SCHUITEVOENDER

Have you ever met a couple that you really enjoyed spending time with? That somehow when they are together they are more than two individuals?

That's who Adam and Angela are to me. They are a young couple with no children. While I enjoy them as individuals, I love seeing them together even more. That's because each of them tends so gently to one another and to their relationship that each becomes more alive, more authentic.

"What would you like for lunch, sweetie?" one says. "I've missed you and we've had so little time recently that I would love to have lunch with you."

"Anything you want to make. I just want to spend a bit of time with you," the other responds.

It is a joy to behold. Whether they are aware of it or not, they have created something larger than themselves—their marriage.

In a new book on the care and tending of relationships, I came across the quote by Connie Zweig and

Neil Schuitevoender. What the authors were referring to was the awareness that in any given relationship, there are three parties: the two of you and the relationship itself, what poet Robert Bly called "the third body," or famous family therapist Carl Whitaker referred to as "the ineffable usness." This entity, say relationship theorists, is as important as either of you and must be tended. If its needs are met, then the two people within the relationship also thrive.

What that made me think about was that for each of us, our relationship, the "usness" or "third body," is as unique as the two individuals that compose it, and it deserves as much gratitude as the people in it. In other words, you don't just want to give thanks for the two of you, but for the "usness" you've created. And the more that you can appreciate this "usness," the more you strengthen your bond.

In a way, each couple in creating the "third body" is actually forming their own culture. A culture with its own customs (like dinner out once a week), rituals (such as the way you do birthdays and holidays), language (including names you have for one another), and stories (like the time your husband stepped in the dog poop in the trailer in the middle of the night and the kids howled with laughter).

What is *your* "usness" like? What customs and rituals have you made together? For my friends Molly and Chuck, it is a large and loving, noisy and chaotic container that holds not only the two of them, but dozens of kids, friends, and other family members that has raucous parties. For Don and me, our "usness" is quiet and peaceable, more tranquil than me on my own, more focused than Don by himself.

Take a minute to think about how you would describe your "third body." Draw a picture of what it looks like. If it ends up a scrawny doodle, ask yourself what you want it to look like and what you might do to make it more like the picture you would like.

Then, think of one way you can celebrate your "usness." One way might be at the celebration of your anniversary—of marriage, or of first meeting or of first recognizing you were in love. Rather than just giving the usual gifts or dinner out, perhaps you can each take a few minutes to say what you give thanks for in particular about your togetherness.

139

$\mathcal{G}$ive Thanks for What's Not Difficult between You

If you suffer greatly when you have a toothache,
it's only right that you be joyful in equal measure
with the "untoothache."

—DAWNA MARKOVA

In doing research for this book, I came across a list of the most common relationship conflicts and problems. Most likely it will sound very familiar to you: money, housework, sex, kids (whether to have them and how to raise them once you've gotten them), and in-laws.

The day I read that list was not the best in the history of Don's and my relationship. I had been traveling a lot, and we were trying to connect for the only time we would see each other for a week. But each of us was feeling annoyed with the other, and we went to sleep without feeling close. I woke in the middle of the night, as I am prone to do now that I'm middle-aged, and, rather than fight it, I began to do background reading for this book. That's when I came across the list.

The first thing I did was to notice which of the items were *not* problems in our relationship: Don and I have no in-law issues at all; we never fight over how to raise Ana Li; I can't remember the last time we've had a cross word over housework. Recognizing that made me feel pretty good about our relationship. Perhaps we weren't doing so badly after all. In fact, I had a lot to be thankful for. Suddenly my heart was flooded with good feelings for him. Before I fell back to sleep, I vowed to express them to Don before I had to leave for the airport at 5 A.M.

Luckily he woke up when my alarm went off. I sat on the edge of the bed and said I was sorry that we had not connected, that I loved him and would miss him while I was gone. He, in turn, expressed that what had been going on for him was that he didn't want me to leave. In that moment, we felt closer than we had in weeks.

I am convinced I would not have made the first move to reconnect if I hadn't read that list. And what it reminds me is this: Sometimes we need a kick-start into gratitude by realizing what is *not* wrong in our relationship. Sometimes we experience thankfulness only when we realize all the ways we could be miserable and are not. That's what my friend Dawna means by the "untoothache"—the joy that is available when we recognize that we are not suffering.

How about you? Take seventeen minutes and write down every relationship problem that people you know or have heard of have. Then circle the ones that are not true for you. Isn't it wonderful that that area of your life is conflict free! Doesn't it feel great to experience the "untoothache"?

Give What You Most Want to Get

If you have only one smile in you, give it to the people you love. Don't be surly at home, then go out in the street and start grinning "Good morning" at total strangers.

—MAYA ANGELOU

I don't know about you, but I suffer from Fear of Going First, particularly as it relates to drawing closer to my husband after an argument. I have been injured, I reason, and therefore he should make the first nice overture. The fact that I feel this way even when we have not been in a fight should be a big clue that something else is going on. Nonetheless, I tend to cling to "You go first" as my basic stance in love: You go first in saying something nice; you go first in reaching out and touching; you go first in doing a sweet thing. Then I'll be nice.

What makes this dynamic so interesting to me is that I have no trouble being sweet, kind, and appreciative to acquaintances and total strangers at the very same time I'm being withholding at home. That's why Maya Angelou's quote hit me so strongly.

Fear of Going First raises its ugly head around the practice of gratitude when I find myself thinking, "I'm not going to be appreciative of *him* until he appreciates *me*."

Sound familiar? A more extreme version of it goes something like this: "No one appreciates me around here. I work my fingers to the bone and no one even notices. And now she wants me to be thankful to those ingrates?"

The answer is, dear one, yes. This is a lesson I've had to learn over and over again, and am still only a beginner at. When it comes to positive attributes like gratitude, kindness, generosity (as opposed to giving material objects such as sweaters or mink coats), the more we give what we want to receive, the more we increase the chances we'll get what we want. When it comes to gratitude, fundamentally you can't lose—offer appreciation and the other person tends to warm toward you, and therefore is more likely to appreciate you in return.

That's because gratitude and positivity build on themselves. Enter into a cycle of thankfulness, and both of you will tend to feel closer and more loving, and therefore more appreciative, closer, and loving.

However it is true that you can't guarantee that the other person will begin to appreciate you more because of your offering. But there is a way you can ensure you get the appreciation you crave—give it to yourself! Many of us crave appreciation from others because we haven't give ourselves enough. We keep looking on the outside for the thanks we need to offer ourselves.

First notice, without judgment, your feelings toward your partner. Do you feel unappreciated? If so, maybe you need to appreciate yourself more. For one week, the first thing in the morning when you wake up, give yourself five specific appreciations. That way you may want gratitude from your partner but won't *need* it. And so you will be more able to receive his or her thanks when it comes your way, and more willing to offer it even if you don't get an immediate response.

147

Remember Your Manners

In spite of the blessing and comfort of a relationship, it isn't a free-for-all. . . . The manners of an emotional relationship are the etiquette of everywhere else, only more so.

—DAPHNE ROSE KINGMA

I was at a friend's house for dinner. This person is the epitome of the gracious hostess, and this evening was no exception. She was wonderfully solicitous of my comfort, warmly thanking me for the bottle of wine I brought. Then her husband joined us in the kitchen, and she instantly changed. "You've got to start the charcoal right away," she demanded. "You know how slow you always are. And make the barbecue sauce correctly this time!" She spoke so harshly that my five-year-old began to cower in the corner.

The worst thing for me personally was that I could see myself in her. Not perhaps quite as sharply, but I too have been guilty of treating the person I love worse than I would a random stranger. I too forget to say "Please" and "Thank you" to the very human being who does more for me than anyone else on the face of the Earth.

I learned this to be true through teaching manners to my daughter. She's been learning to say "Please" and

"Thank you" for a couple years now, and recently has begun to observe that while Don and I are vigilant about making her say both, we frequently forget with one another.

What is it that allows us to think that the rules of etiquette don't apply to the ones who are closest to us? What made my friend think that her husband wasn't deserving of a "Please would you start the charcoal now?" and "Thank you for making the sauce"? Is it because we see one another's contributions as their "job," their family obligation that is undeserving of appreciation?

Even required jobs are worthy of thanks, maybe even more so. My friend Ann once told me that her father thanked her mother for cooking dinner every evening of their married life. Despite that, as a stay-at-home housewife, it was her job, he graciously thanked her every single evening. One can only hope that she found ways to thank him for going to work every day.

When we drop our pleases and thank yous, we can too easily become blind to all that we are receiving from our beloved, and we lessen in him or her the desire to give. When we include "Please" and "Thank you," either through written notes, a thankful hug, or the words, two wonderful things occur: We remind ourselves exactly what favors we are asking for and receiving, which increases our sense of gratitude, and, by acknowledging his or her contribution, we create the possibility that our mate will continue to love and assist us.

Try this. Keep track of your manners toward your spouse for three days. Just notice whether you write or say "Please" and "Thank you" on a regular basis. If the answer is yes, great! If not, you can change that by asking yourself, "How would I act right now if this were a business acquaintance I wanted to impress?" Practice expressing pleases and thank yous for a week, and see if your relationship changes for the better.

Share What Makes You Feel Appreciated

*I know, indeed, of nothing more subtly satisfying and
cheering than a knowledge of the real good will and
appreciation of others. Such happiness does not come with
money, nor does it flow from fine physical state. It cannot
be bought. But it is the keenest joy, after all; and the
toiler's truest and best reward.*

—WILLIAM DEAN HOWELLS

I have a friend who is a genius at gratitude. What makes
her so good at it is that she pays close attention to
what each person is doing and notes it very specifically
in her appreciations. And she's great at figuring out *how*
the other person likes to be appreciated. To one friend
she gives a beautiful card, to another a dinner on the
town, to yet another a vase. As a consequence of her
precise appreciations, her friends and loved ones all feel
greatly loved by her. Indeed, I would say she is the most
loving person I know.

I am going to suggest that we all become like my
friend by getting specific about what makes us feel appreciated and sharing that awareness with our partner.

The reason for this is that as human beings, it is as if
we speak different languages when it comes to feeling

loved. Just as we want to learn another person's language to better communicate with them, so do we want to teach him or her our language so that we can enhance our experience of gratitude as much as possible. That's because it's always easy to think in our own language without having to translate. So, for instance, while it's important to be able to say to yourself, "When my spouse says I look tired, he's saying how much he appreciates all I do for him," for you gratitude that comes in the form of a bouquet of flowers may be more effective. And the more we know how to be effective in our gratitude and appreciation of one another, the more we increase the likelihood that we will experience the upswell of feeling that gratitude brings us. Otherwise, we may spend a lot of time and energy expressing thanks in ways that are difficult for the other to receive.

So this practice is really simple. Just make a list of all the things that make you feel thanked. Tops on my list would be flowers, a dinner out, a written note, a day in bed to read. What's on your list?

When you share your lists with one another, do so in the spirit of connection, not obligation. This should not become something the other *has* to do or you will fly into a rage or a pout. This is just ways you really know that you are appreciated that you want to share to help your partner speak your language.

Receive What's Being Given

You are always being given opportunities to love and be loved, yet ask yourself how many times in your life you have squandered these opportunities.

—GARY ZUKAV

When I was growing up, I had an aunt and uncle, Judy and Mike, who I saw very infrequently. But every time we got together, my aunt would spend the whole time complaining to my mother that her husband didn't love or appreciate her. He seemed like a nice guy to me, so as I got older, I paid closer attention to the two of them to try and figure it out. Because we were family, we spent a lot of holidays together, and I began to notice that no matter what Mike got her for Christmas—a diamond pendant, a ruby ring, a frilly negligee, a vase, or cozy socks—Judy would find a way to criticize it (the necklace: "Where would I wear such a thing; you never take me anywhere"; the vase: "Not romantic enough"; the nightgown "I'm too fat."). She was incapable of seeing what Mike was trying to say with his gifts. Mike also gave quite a number of compliments to Judy—"You look divine tonight, dear," "What a great job you did on that project"—which she similarly discounted.

As I said in a previous chapter, I've come to see this problem as one of low self-esteem: we have to feel worthy to receive the love and attention that is being offered, or else we are not aware it is coming our way. But it also has to do with having certain mindsets that get in the way of actually seeing what we are receiving. If you only recognize appreciation if it comes in written form, for instance, and your partner is always saying nice things to you but never writes anything down, you can be oblivious to what you're being given. If love means roses to you and your mate gets you daffodils, you can easily discount the gift.

The truth is our partners are giving to us all the time, and we need to be tuned in enough so that we can consciously receive the gift. This has often been characterized in gender terms—she wants words and he fixes the washing machine to show he cares—but it actually cuts across those lines. We each notice what we are set up to notice.

But one of the skills in the practice of gratitude is becoming more and more aware of precisely what we are receiving in all domains. Just for a moment, take some time to reflect on what your mate does all the time on your behalf to show his or her appreciation of you. It may help to ask him or her what those things are, because they might be invisible to you. Or ask a friend who knows you both what he or she thinks you are being given. Then make a commitment to yourself to acknowledge the meaning behind the action or words next time they occur; for example, "Oh, thanks for folding the laundry without my asking. You know how happy it makes me feel to not have to nag"; or "When you rub my feet you are telling me how thankful you are for all the work I've done, aren't you?"

The more we can receive what our mate is giving, the more the river of appreciation will flow between us.

157

Ꙋo the 5 to 1

In successful relationships, there is a
five to one ratio of positive to negative comments.

—DAWNA MARKOVA, CITING RESEARCH BY
JOHN GOTTMAN AND OTHERS

If ever there was a case for an attitude of gratitude in love, it can be found in the research on long-term relationships that shows that in happy couplings, the number of positive to negative comments are 5 to 1. Not only that, but if you do want to request some kind of behavior change, employing the 5-to-1 ratio greatly increases the possibility that you will be heard.

For someone who truly believed complaining was the way to get my needs met, this has been a true stunner: You mean it's not effective to say what's wrong all the time? I thought that was the best way to get problems solved.

It turns out, naturally enough, that the other person gets defensive when negative comments are made, and so is less amiable to even hearing what you have to say, much less changing his or her behavior. However, when you employ five appreciative comments *before* the negative, receptivity is increased.

The positive comments have to be sincere and heartfelt, of course, to be effective, and you can't bombard the other person all day long with requests for changes couched in the 5 to 1 framework. But overall, for relationship happiness, there needs to be five times as much positivity as negativity!

This is a great argument for the practice of gratitude, for the more you openly appreciate one another, the more the positive ratio goes up and the greater possibility for long-term contentment. Begin by getting a sense of what the ratio is right now. On a piece of paper, make three columns: Positive (like "It was so wonderful of you to run to the store for me"), Negative (such as "Why do you always forget what I've told you?"), and Neutral (like "It's raining out"). For a week, track your comments to your mate by simply making a tick in each column whenever you say anything. At the end of the week, count up the ticks. What's your ratio? If it can use improvement, note that without beating yourself up; make a commitment to be more positive, and continue to track.

Give Thanks for Being Loved with All Your Foibles

We love those who know the worst of us
and don't turn their faces away.

—WALKER PERCY

One of the best ways that I've discovered to practice gratitude in love is to take an objective look at myself, with all my flaws and foibles, and realize that despite all of them, Don still loves me. How amazing! How wonderful! Even though I can lose my temper, even though I have a tendency to overgeneralize when angry, even though I can get so absorbed in my work that I forget everything and everyone else, he still loves me.

Each of us who is privileged to be loved by a special someone is the recipient of this incredible gift—the love of someone who, in Walker Percy's words, knows the worst of us and still stays with us. Still includes us in their loving regard, still bathes us in a pool of acceptance, still stands by our side and on our side.

This is not to say we should use this as an excuse to behave badly, for everyone has his or her limits. But it is to acknowledge how very lucky we are to be loved in spite of our flaws, despite our mistakes, despite our failures to grow and change. When we become truly aware of the miracle of that loving acceptance, we can't help but be overcome with a profound sense of thankfulness—to the person who offers us that mercy, and to the relationship itself, where we can sink into the truth of who we are in all its beauty and challenges.

A simple way to do this is to make a list, either on paper, on tape, or in your mind of your specific behaviors that are difficult for others. In doing this, please use compassion rather than condemnation, awareness rather than judgment. This is not a chance to beat yourself up, but rather a quiet, realistic truth telling about the baggage you bring to a relationship: I have two children from a previous relationship who have a lot of problems; I can get very stubborn about even the smallest things; I can say hurtful things without thinking; I put my work above my relationship; I tend to always put my own needs first. Whatever is true for you, note it.

Then, recognize that you, a very human being, flawed as we all are, are loved and valued by the special person in your life. Is that an absolute miracle?

And so that you are sure not to use this list to punish yourself, make another list of behaviors entitled: All the Ways I Am Incredible. Put them down: I'm great at supporting the growth of those I love; I'm wonderful in a crisis; I'm steadfast in my work so my family doesn't have to worry about income. . . . Now, in the context of this list, appreciate yourself for the miraculous being you are. Isn't your partner fortunate to have you in his or her life?

THE PRACTICE
OF GRATITUDE
IN LOVE

Recall Your Love Story

I've found 94 percent of the time that couples
who put a positive spin on their marriage's history
are likely to have a happy future as well.

—JOHN GOTTMAN

Whenever my friend Dawna's at a dinner party where she is getting to know the people present, she always asks people to tell their love stories. From spending time with her, I've gotten into the habit too. There's just something romantic and wonderful about hearing how other people managed to pick one another out from among the 6 billion people on the Earth. I've heard poignant stories, funny stories, dramatic stories. The only thing they seem to have in common is that telling them tends to bring the couple closer together, at least for a moment, as they begin to articulate what it was about the other person that caught their fancy. I suddenly notice tender glances between them; one may reach for the other's hand; they finish one another's sentences in a happy, connected way.

While I noticed these effects, I had no idea until recently that marriage researchers actually use how a couple tells their story as predictors of breaking up or staying together. That makes sense, particularly in the context of gratitude in love. When we tell the story in such a way that we emphasize all the positives in the situation, we are adding to our emotional reserve bank account of love and appreciation: Yes, it was great how you came up to me the day after we met and said you loved me. Yes, it was great that you brought me a flower from the hedge outside and asked me to dance.

Researcher and couples therapist John Gottman has found the positive effects of telling your love story so strong that he uses it with couples whose relationships are in trouble as a way of rekindling positive feelings. In truth, the practice is no different than any of those for sparking a sense of gratitude—it just wakes us up once again to the wonderful things we've been taking for granted. But because courtship is such a magical time, it's particularly effective in fostering appreciation and thankfulness.

So if you need a jumpstart on gratefulness, how about sharing your love story? Tell it to your kids (kids love parent stories), or do as my friend does and introduce it as a dinner party topic; most everyone will appreciate that. Or bring it up in an intimate moment between just the two of you.

Whenever you do it, pay close attention to the ways

you loved one another in the beginning. Those may be things you still cherish but have become inured to. Pick them out, dust them off, and watch the sparkle between you glow even more.

Don't Forget the Bad Old Days

Nostalgia isn't what it used to be.

—ANONYMOUS

Last night I was fixing dinner, waiting for Don to come home. It was ten minutes before six. I knew that he would either be there by six or call, because that was our agreement with one another. Suddenly I recalled how in my last relationship, I had spent hundreds of hours wondering where my partner was and when he was going to come home. He would bristle at having to "report in" and hated feeling controlled in any way. But being left in limbo was really hard on me. I would progress from wonder to worry to panic. I realized that in ten years, Don had never given me one minute's worry on that score, and I was suddenly flooded with such a feeling of appreciation and love that it brought tears to my eyes.

Because we have a tendency to take for granted what is right in front of us, remembering the "bad old days" is one of the ways to recall what is wonderful about our relationship right now. What I mean by the bad old days is the time before the relationship we are currently in. When we were sick of the dating scene or the string of nights alone; when we were stuck in a bad dynamic in another relationship; when we were longing for love.

This is not necessarily easy. We humans often have a tendency to romanticize the past as swiftly as we criticize the present. That's what nostalgia is, what novelist Milan Kundera called "the unbearable lightness of being"—the human tendency to minimize the pain and suffering of the past and paint it instead in rosy hues of "the good old days." Rather than remembering how much we hated dating, we recall how fun it was to be footloose and fancy-free. Rather than remembering all the nights of waiting for the man to come home, we only recall what a brilliant mind he had and how great our conversations were.

Nostalgia is such a human emotion that we also can get nostalgic for the past of our current relationship— "Oh, it was so much fun when we first got together, not boring like now"—forgetting entirely, for instance, how he spent the first six months deciding whether to pick you or go back to his old girlfriend.

To counteract the tendency toward nostalgia, which is nothing more than an overvaluing of the past and an undervaluing the present, it's helpful to remember at least every so often just what it was about our previous state that was so difficult and painful. That way we can wake up to this present moment, more able to live in gratefulness for the fullness of the love present in today.

Take a moment right now to think: What is better than it was before you met this person? Can you express that to him or her?

Notice Repair Attempts

He who cannot forgive others breaks the bridge over which
he must pass himself.

—GEORGE HERBERT

Author James Hewitt tells a story in his book *Illustrations Unlimited* that goes like this: A Spanish father and his teenage son have a terrible falling out, and the boy runs away. The father searches for him everywhere, to no avail. Finally he runs an ad in the main newspaper in Madrid that reads, "Dear Paco, meet me in front of the newspaper office at noon. All is forgiven. I love you. Your father."

"The next day at noon in front of the newspaper office," writes Hewitt, "800 'Pacos' show up. They were all seeking forgiveness and love from their fathers."

Each and every one of us in a relationship needs forgiveness from one another from time to time. No matter our intentions, we wound each other in myriad ways. In order to keep the stream of gratitude flowing, we must be able to find our way back to one another.

However, for whatever reasons, not everyone will be able to say, "I'm sorry, please forgive me." But all of us do find ways to reach out and try to mend relationship breeches when they happen. Relationship experts call these "repair attempts," a term I love because it acknowledges that a tear has occurred in the fabric of your love and that you want to fix it somehow. Repair attempts include requests for forgiveness, but they also can include a silent hand reaching out to touch yours, a joke, a smile, a "You may have a point." Just about anything that tries to bring the two of you back together can be classified as a repair attempt.

My husband is a genius at repair attempts. One of his greatest is a hyperbolic statement that he is all wrong and I'm all right, said with a goofy grin that I can't resist. Inevitably in response I find myself saying, "No, no, I played a part as well," and soon we are back on track together.

Repair attempts are very significant, because if you ignore too many times a proffered hand of reconnection, the chance to come back together eventually disappears. Researchers have found that those on the verge of breakup ignore their partner's repair attempts or even use them to escalate an argument.

No matter how happy your relationship, you will hurt one another and need to find ways to come back together. It helps if you each understand how the other does it, so you will recognize the signals when they are given.

Take a few moments to think about your repair attempts. What do you do to signal that you are sorry or want to reconcile? I, for instance, always say, "I don't want to be in a fight." Share your list, and ask your mate to let you know what he or she does. Then vow to look at these behaviors in their true light—ways of saying, "Let's be close again."

Appreciate Love's Obligations

*Obligations and responsibilities are an important compo-
nent of a good life; they are not merely burdens.*

—BO LOZOFF

I have an older friend who became a widow a couple
years ago. In speaking with her about how she was ad-
justing, she said, "You know, I really miss having someone to fuss over. When Jim was alive, I hated all the
cooking and cleaning, the boring stuff of domestic life.
Now I just wish I had someone to do all that for."

As my friend experienced, loss is often a powerful
trigger for retroactive gratitude. Too often we don't appreciate our good health until we lose it, or even life itself unless we have a near-death experience. We humans
often need the wake-up call of loss to recognize the
beauty of what we have.

One place where we can use this tendency to our
advantage is with duties and obligations. It's easy to see
our family duties as burdens, things that we have to do.
From this place, we tend to perform these tasks be-
grudgingly, resentfully, or passive-aggressively.

But when we view these things as ways we show our love to those we share our lives with, they get elevated out of the humdrum and take on much more meaning. And when we add to that the awareness that we are privileged to have someone to do them for, then we are really flying with the angels.

That's why, when I find myself getting resentful about something I have to do for my family, I remind myself that I am grateful that I have them to do it for. This isn't a "trick"; I really am grateful. I have lived alone and know what it's like to have no one to cook for, to run to the store for, to fuss over on birthdays.

When we appreciate love's obligations, we recognize that not only is it a gift to be loved, but it is an honor to have someone to be loving toward. The river of love in us wants to move both ways—yes, we want to be loved, but we also need a chance to show our lovingness. When we have the opportunity, that is something to be truly grateful for.

For one week, practice looking at the obligations love requires of you as gifts rather than burdens. How do you feel at the end of the week? More energized rather than burned out? More connected rather than angry?

$\mathcal{T}$ake a Daily Gratitude Vow

The whole problem with people is . . . that they
know what matters, but they don't choose it.

—SUE MONK KIDD

In his book *It's a Meaningful Life*, Bo Lozoff describes how he and his wife of thirty years take a marriage vow every day. First thing in the morning, they sit down, hold hands, look into one another's eyes, and say, "May I truly cherish you today, knowing this may be our last day together."

That practice really struck me because I've been doing a bit of thinking about vows. Coming from the counterculture '60s, I pretty much avoided the whole thing for a long time. But seven years ago, I got married, and I must say I've taken my wedding vows very seriously. In fact, we have them hanging in our bedroom, and in conflict, the worst thing one of us can say to the other is that we're not living up to those vows. So I guess they are powerful in motivating action.

Since then, I've seen several books about using vows to support a change you want to make in your life and have talked to many people who have taken vows of all sorts. The power of vows, I've come to see, lies in that they are consciously chosen and then publicly stated. I used to think they were some kind of inviolate border, which, if you crossed, you would be punished. But I've come to understand that for many people they indicate a direction a person wants to move in, and the seriousness of their commitment to that direction.

I've even begun to use them myself and with clients, to great success—as long as people don't use them to beat themselves up when they forget or slip up. So with that as a caveat, the practice I am going to suggest here is a gratitude vow. You can do it together, like Bo and Sita, or you can do it just for yourself. The idea is to make real your commitment to focus on what is good and right in your relationship, rather than getting too bogged down in its flaws. The Lozoff's vow includes the possibility of death, which you may or may not be comfortable with. Recognizing the impermanence of everything and everyone is one way to wake ourselves out of habit and really focus on the beauty in our life. It is true that this day may be your last with your beloved— about 200,000 people die every day, some young, many without warning. Consciously recognizing that may help you not take him or her for granted.

But that might be too difficult for you to do, and that's OK. The exact words to use should be yours. It should be something that you are really willing to make a commitment to. I suggest that you try doing the same vow for at least a week and notice what effect it has on you and your relationship. If you find it helpful in keeping your focus on the good, great. If not, try something else.

Express Your Appreciation to Others

There are never enough "I love you's."

—LENNY BRUCE

A funny thing happened to me after the breakup of my fourteen-year relationship. I met someone who knew my ex, and we got to talking. At some point it became clear that she thought *I* dumped *him* because he was so full of praise of me in his conversation that she couldn't believe he would say those positive things if he had left me. In fact, the ending was his choosing. After I cleared up the confusion, I remember thinking, If only he had said those things while we were still together.

This incident still lingers with me ten years later. One reason, I think, is that it illustrates how wonderful it is to hear yourself talked about positively in the third person. Since then, I've paid attention whenever people talk about their sweethearts' great qualities. It doesn't happen that often, at least in the circles I hang around in. We tend to bond with one another over our complaints about our spouses, rather than by sharing all the great things about them.

But does it have to be that way? What if we were to broadcast to the world all the ways our partner was wonderful? Any number of great things would begin to happen. First, we would be reminded ourselves, which we tend to need. Second, our partner can bask in the glow of our regard, which feels great. Third, we will encourage those around us to do the same, changing an atmosphere of apathy or negativity into one that's glowing with the power of positive thinking.

Try it for yourself and see what happens. At a dinner party or some other public gathering, find an occasion to speak of your sweetheart in the third person so that he or she can overhear. Make it seem like a secret that you are telling.

Learning happens after we try something new and pause to notice its effect. So be sure to stop after you try this a few times, and evaluate what the effect was. If you like it, keep doing it.

We worry too much about people getting swelled heads. Genuine praise and appreciation is some of the best medicine in the world for self-concept, self-esteem, and self-worth. As Lenny Bruce said, "There are never enough 'I love you's," so don't worry about overdosing.

Ask a Friend for Help

Some people think only intellect counts: knowing how to
solve problems, knowing how to get by, knowing how
to identify an advantage and seize it. But the functions
of intellect are insufficient without courage, love,
friendship, compassion, and empathy.

—DEAN KOONTZ

About ten years ago, a friend of mine was in a terrible place in her relationship. She called me up and said, "I'm not sure I can go on. Everything looks so bleak between us. I don't think we're in love anymore." Because this friend had been generally happy in her relationship, what I said in response was this, "I'm sorry you are hurting and things look so terrible. I'm thinking of all that you have loved and appreciated in your relationship, and I'm holding the possibility of its future until you can again."

As it turned out, she and her husband found their way through that dark night of their relationship and have been together ever since. But what's been so interesting about this incident for me is that she has referred to it dozens of times since, saying that it was my belief in her relationship that allowed her to get through and see the good in it again.

Sometimes we can get so mired down with one another in our intimate relationships that we lose all perspective. We simply can't recall anything we love or appreciate about the other; we have serious doubts over whether it is even worth preserving the relationship. That's where a friend may come in handy. Someone you can call up and say, "Remind me why I love this so-and-so." Or, "Tell me again all the great things I have told you over the years about her so I can remember." Or, "What do you see that is good in my relationship?"

Intimate relationships can strain all our personal emotional and spiritual resources, despite our best intentions. We can and do hurt, insult, anger, and devastate one another. We can reach the end of our proverbial rope. That's when its important to have someone outside the dyad to remind us of the gifts that we are receiving, the joy that we have experienced together, so that we can regain a sense of perspective and decide from a more balanced place whether we should continue on together.

I hope you are not in the place of needing a friend for this right now. But it's useful as a practice to think about who you might call on if and when you need such support. Pick someone who really knows and appreciates the two of you, not just someone who will support whatever mood you happen to be in. You are looking for someone who will remind you of your relationship's beauty while not diminishing the difficulties you are experiencing. If no one comes to mind, be that friend for yourself. While in a place of gratitude and appreciation, write a letter to yourself about everything you love about your mate. Then put it in a place where you can find it if you need to.

When Times Get Tough, Go to the Higher Level

No one is wise enough by himself.

—TITUS MACCIUS PLAUTUS

A friend of mine says that the point of being alive is a quest toward wholeness, and that we tend to fall in love with a person who represents our unlived parenthesis. In other words, we are a certain configuration of characteristics that lean in a certain direction, like one parenthesis, and the person we choose for our own tends to lean in the other direction, like the second parenthesis. Together we make a whole as we each try to incorporate the unlived parenthesis into ourselves.

This point of view is comforting to me when times get tough in my relationship. Sometimes the only gratefulness practice I can do is to look at the lessons I'm learning and be grateful for the learning. Relationships are not just a bed of roses; we may be beset by all kinds of challenges—job loss, addictions, death of loved ones, affairs, money woes, and the like. These are not easy things to live through, alone or together.

And within the life cycle of a relationship there are seasons to negotiate—happy ones like the spring of new love and the blossoming of summer, but also difficult ones like the fall of stagnation and boredom, the winter of bleak discontent. We may not make it—50 percent of all relationships end in divorce, and the statistics are even higher for second- and third-time marriages.

It is precisely because intimate relationships are so challenging that they are some of the best places for soulmaking. Within the container of love, two souls must grow qualities they never dreamed they could— things like patience, fortitude, resiliency, flexibility, stamina. Emotional maturity. Generosity of spirit.

For each of us, what we must learn is different, but learn and grow we must if we are to survive together. And within this context, where gratitude can be found is precisely in the challenges themselves. For it is because we have suffered that we have grown.

It takes nobility of soul to go to this higher level when times are tough between us, to seek out the hidden blessings within the pain we may be experiencing. When we do this, we are not trying to minimize the pain or Pollyanna it away. We are simply acknowledging that the two experiences run alongside one another: the difficulty and our thankfulness for how the difficulty has made us better.

Looking at this is not easy, but it is fruitful. If you are going though a dark night of your relationship right now, take a few moments to journal about what soul lessons you've been learning. And if you aren't facing some difficulty right in this moment, perhaps you can look back at the past to when you were. What did you learn? To stand up for yourself more? To reach out to others for help? To cut the other person some slack? That you were stronger than you thought? Whatever it is, acknowledge and give thanks for the lesson. For it is precisely where we have been wounded that the light shines through us most strongly.

It is my prayer that when times are tough between you, you will hold your relationship in this higher awareness, as a sacred container for soulmaking, and as such, experience it as worthy of your thankfulness.

191

THE JOYFUL JOURNEY

The size of your body is of little account;
the size of your brain is of much account;
the size of your heart is of the most
account of all.

—B. C. FORBES

I love this quote by Forbes. It never fails to remind me of what, ultimately, matters the most to me. Those of us who are in ongoing intimate relationships are privileged to have the opportunity to grow the size of our hearts on a daily basis. We grow them by our looking at the soul lessons our love life is offering us; we grow them by the continual experience of taking another human being into account. And we also grow them by experiencing the joy that comes from being deeply seen and known and offering that same gift to our beloved.

Each and every relationship offers many opportunities for joy, if we but seize the chances we are given on a regular basis to be thankful. Thankfulness is actually the mother of joy, for it is only when we register that we are receiving something wonderful that we experience the surge of positive feeling we know as joy. If we do not take time to be grateful, we tend to experience life and love as same old, same old. Without gratefulness, we can too easily become numb. Gratefulness in love wakes us up to all that is precious and beautiful, and grows our hearts larger still.

To open ourselves to the full joy that is possible from our most intimate relationships is a sacred honor. But it is not something we do once and for all. Hearts open and close, rightly so. Practicing gratitude in love is just that—a practice. Like all other soul practices, we can get better and better at it, but there is no discernable endpoint. All there is is the practice. We try and our hearts fill with joy. We get hurt and shut down for a while. Then we begin again. We set our feet on the path of gratefulness and continue the journey.

May you enjoy to the fullest the journey of love you are on, and may you experience its blessings on a daily basis.

MY THANKS

Words seem so inadequate for the sense of great-fullness I feel when I think of my teachers Daphne Rose Kingma and Dawna Markova. All of what you see on these pages reflect in some way what I have learned from them about love and thankfulness. Given the specific nature of this book, Daphne's teachings, as articulated in *365 Days of Love, True Love,* and *A Lifetime of Love,* form the undercurrent of my understanding about the nature of love relationships. And whatever richness and dimension the practices suggested here have is through the grace of Dawna, the goddess of development practices.

I also give profound thanks to my husband Donald McIlraith, who graciously allowed me to reveal our relationship with its warts and foibles as well as its beauties and joys, and to my daughter Ana Li, who continues to be a daily teacher of joy and appreciation.

Thanks too to all those readers who have written to me about their practice of gratitude, to my clients who practice with me, and to my teachers at a distance whose books help inform these pages of ideas beyond my own. I think especially of the work of John Gottman, particularly as it is articulated in *The Seven*

Principles for Making Marriage Work, Rachel Naomi Remen in *My Grandfather's Blessing*, Darlene Cohen in *Finding a Joyful Life in the Heart of Pain*, Bo Lozoff in *It's a Meaningful Life*, and Sue Patton Thoele in *The Woman's Book of Courage*, *The Woman's Book of Confidence*, and *The Woman's Book of Soul*. And thanks once again to David Cooperrider's work on appreciative inquiry and to Brother David Stendl-Rast, whose perspective on gratitude helped set me off on this journey in the first place.

ABOUT THE AUTHOR

Bestselling author M. J. Ryan is the former CEO and cofounder of Conari Press in Berkeley, California. One of the creators of the bestselling Random Acts of Kindness™ series (over one million copies in print), she is the author of *Attitudes of Gratitude*, *The Giving Heart*, *365 Health and Happiness Boosters*, and, under the *nom de plume* Susannah Seton, the *Simple Pleasures* series. She is also the editor of the award-winning book *The Fabric of the Future* and of *A Grateful Heart*.

She is currently a consultant with Professional Thinking Partners, where she specializes in coaching senior-level executives, small business owners, entrepreneurs, and other professionals on issues of life purpose, leadership development, and collaborative thinking. She is also one of the facilitators of TimeOut, a five-day bimonthly retreat on personal renewal for corporate executives and other professionals at Robert Redford's resort in Sundance, Utah. A popular speaker and workshop leader on what she calls "the modern virtues"— simplicity, gratitude, generosity, and kindness—her work has appeared in numerous newspapers and magazines, including *USA Today*, *Family Circle*, *Ladies Home Journal*, *Yoga Journal*, and *Body & Soul*. Visit her Web site at www.maryjaneryan.com.

To Our Readers

CONARI PRESS publishes books on topics ranging from spirituality, personal growth, and relationships to women's issues, parenting, and social issues. Our mission is to publish quality books that will make a difference in people's lives—how we feel about ourselves and how we relate to one another. We value integrity, compassion, and receptivity, both in the books we publish and in the way we do business.

As a member of the community, we donate our damaged books to nonprofit organizations, dedicate a portion of our proceeds from certain books to charitable causes, and continually look for new ways to use natural resources as wisely as possible.

Our readers are our most important resource, and we value your input, suggestions, and ideas about what you would like to see published. Please feel free to contact us, to request our latest book catalog, or to be added to our mailing list.

Conari Press
An imprint of Red Wheel/Weiser, LLC
P.O. Box 612
York Beach, ME 03910-0612
800-423-7087
www.conari.com

Enjoy These Other Products from M.J. Ryan

Attitudes of Gratitude   The Giving Heart   365 Health and
Happiness Boosters

Attitudes of Gratitude Journal, Boxed Note Set, and Inspirational Cards

To order:
Call Toll-Free: 800-423-7087